STUDIO GRACE

Also by Eric Siblin

*The Cello Suites: J. S. Bach, Pablo Casals, and the
Search for a Baroque Masterpiece*

STUDIO GRACE

THE MAKING OF A RECORD

ERIC SIBLIN

ANANSI

This edition published in 2015 by
House of Anansi Press Inc.
110 Spadina Avenue, Suite 801
Toronto, ON, M5V 2K4
Tel. 416-363-4343
Fax 416-363-1017
www.houseofanansi.com

House of Anansi Press is committed to protecting our natural
environment. As part of our efforts, the interior of this book is printed on
paper that contains 100% post-consumer recycled fibres, is acid-free, and is
processed chlorine-free.

19 18 17 16 15   1 2 3 4 5

Library and Archives Canada Cataloguing in Publication

Siblin, Eric, author
Studio Grace : the making of a record / by Eric Siblin.

Issued in print and electronic formats.
ISBN 978-1-77089-934-6 (bound). — ISBN 978-1-77089-935-3 (html)

1. Siblin, Eric, 1960–. 2. Sound recordings — Production and
direction. 3. Popular music — Canada — 2011–2020. I. Title.

ML410.S564A3 2015   780.92   C2015-900818-2
                                           C2015-900819-0

Book design: Alysia Shewchuk

We acknowledge for their financial support of our publishing program
the Canada Council for the Arts, the Ontario Arts Council, and the Government
of Canada through the Canada Book Fund.

Printed and bound in Canada

For Herbert Elliot Siblin

TABLE OF CONTENTS

The songs featured in this book can be streamed or down-loaded at ericsiblin.com. Enter the access code: Papyrus. The website is expected to be active by mid-March 2015.

"In a word, it is so powerful a thing that it ravisheth the soul, the queen of the senses, by sweet pleasure (which is an happy cure); and corporall tunes pacifie our incorporeall soul and carries it beyond it self, helps, elevates, extends it."

—Robert Burton, "The Secret Power of Musick" (1621)

CHORUS INTERRUPTUS

A**NOTHER SONG GOT AWAY** last night. It slipped through my fingers, escaped the chord structures, and made a clean break from the fretboard. Guitar strings were power-less to rein in the melody. Even now, the half-finished song dares me to pluck sound out of thin air and pin down its essence.

I was trying to finish a chorus for the song I call "Grace of Love." You can't force these things. But neither can you sit on your hands waiting for the Muse to strum some strings.

It is the fault of Morey, my perfectionist mentor, forever spurring me on to greater heights, places I cannot quite reach; and Jo, my capricious sounding board, who is rarely satisfied; and the velvet-voiced singers who tried their hands at the song, from Rebecca to Shaharah; and Bilerman the producer, who led me to believe that my music was worthy; and finally, I hold my father accountable, for he, when he was at death's door, put the idea of the song in my head.

There are many other songs. If "Grace of Love" is still minus its elusive chorus when I get to the studio, it will not be overly missed. But the anguish caused by this unfinished tune is typical. The songs have not come easy.

HOW LONG HAVE YOU BEEN GONE?

F OR A LONG TIME songs had been percolating in me. I
dealt with them as best I could. But a new urgency had
recently been brought to the equation. I wasn't sure why. A
breakup had led me to struggle mightily with a song that
became known as "Country Mile." It was missing a chorus,
but after countless attempts I figured it out and a weight was
lifted. Other tunes were in various states of incompletion. I
wanted to finish them all.

Then came my chance encounters with Morey Richman
and Jo Simonetti. I met them both, on separate occasions,
at the same Montreal café: Morey, a face from my distant
past; Jo, a new visage that I wanted to gaze upon in my
immediate future.

She was wearing a red woollen cap and tapping away
on a laptop. I found myself at a table nearby and struck up a
conversation that grew into a long conversation. Jo's face lit

up when she broke into a smile. She was attractive to begin with, but it was as if all her constituent parts—wide brown eyes, high cheekbones, aquiline nose, shoulder-length dark hair—were lying dormant until a smile switched on their collective beauty. It was a long while before she referred to a husband.

One week later, we crossed paths again in the same Starbucks and had another caffeinated chat. My ear was tuned to the nuances of her marital status. The moment of truth came when she asked if I'd ever been married.

"Nope," I said. "I missed that train."

"Some of us were on it and jumped off," she said.

"Really? I thought you said last week that you had a husband?"

"Ex-husband."

"Oh."

"Yes, there's that little ex in there."

My ears playing tricks on me, as usual.

"I guess I misheard you."

I sent her an email later that afternoon: "I know this is ridiculously last-minute, but seeing as you've suddenly become single would you like to have dinner tonight?"

"Funny," she replied, "becoming single did not feel very sudden."

As things turned out, we were to remain unattached. Coupling up was just not in the cards for us, though we discovered something else that brought us very close together.

Jo was a classically trained piano player, with a mellifluous, delicate singing voice. Plus she composed a few songs.

Although I had a nice touch on guitar and could write decent songs, or so I thought, my downfall had always been my subpar vocals. On occasion, in the right key and style, I sounded passable, or at least true to the song. But I was forever on the lookout for a good singer.

I had a piano at my place, and we started playing music together, Jo on lead vocals and piano, me on acoustic guitar. Except for one of her originals ("How Long Have You Been Gone?") they were all my compositions, the dozen or so tunes that had been floating and percolating and clamouring to get out.

Jo was not shy about passing judgement. Lose a bridge here; add a chord there. Her suggestions were always discerning. She was good chorus karma for my songs. She sang the ones that worked, protesting occasionally that one of my melodies was too "masculine" or contained a word like *papyrus* or just rubbed her the wrong way.

She had diva tendencies. There were occasions when she refused to sing without a bottle of Stella Artois or a snack of pomegranate seeds. She also had bad memories of being treated "like a trained seal" at the family piano when she was growing up.

Eventually, Jo purchased an electric piano and went on a composing binge of her own. She had no desire to hitch her star to my clunky wagonload of songs. And she was a star, or about to become one. I was certain of it.

Still, she was a godsend for my songs, lending an expert ear that I came to trust almost without question.

CLOUDBURST

I WROTE MY FIRST song at the age of thirteen, an instrumental tune in C major, complete with a verse and a chorus. It was called "Cloudburst."

I had decided at the age of eleven or so that I wanted to play guitar. I'm not sure why. My parents were not musicians. My mother took piano lessons as a child, but I never saw her fingers touch ivory. Still, she has a good ear and a natural sense of rhythm and gravitates to music. My first father, who died young, was a sports car racer who liked the jazz vocals of Lena Horne. My mother remarried, and my new father, an upbeat accountant, played Beethovenesque and marching-type material on the stereo system in his den with the sliding door tightly shut, part of his constant battle to obtain peace and quiet from four kids.

My enthusiasm for guitar must have been on account of bands like the Monkees and the Partridge Family that I saw on television in the 1970s. My parents were not opposed to the idea, and I soon found myself with a cheap acoustic guitar and a teacher named Ted.

I vividly remember plucking the notes for "When the Saints Go Marching In" on a camel-coloured tweed sofa sometime after one of my lessons. I had the pleasant feeling that I was impressing my younger brother with my new-found skills, as if it were some magic trick I'd conjured. But the guitar lessons did not last long.

About a year later I had a bar mitzvah, and the most exciting gift to come my way was from my aunt and uncle: a stereo system. On the back of the amplifier were several inputs. One of them was intriguingly labelled *Elec. Guitar.* I thought: *What? Can this be what I think it is? I can plug an electric guitar into this baby?*

Among my other gifts was a seventy-dollar gift certificate to the Eaton's department store. I knew exactly what to do with it. I took the bus downtown and made my way to the music section of the store. For sixty-nine dollars I was able to buy a guitar, though not a case to go with it. I left Eaton's with a cardboard box that contained an anonymous-looking white-finish solid-body electric guitar. Back home, I plugged it in the *Elec. Guitar* input. The sound was instantly pleasurable.

I formed a band not long afterwards. By that time, my head was filled with more than television ditties. I'd acquired several records that I took a liking to, some as gifts, some as hand-me-downs. There was Traffic, the Rolling Stones, the Who, and the Doors.

Blending the rudimentary techniques I remembered from Ted's lessons with the new music in my head, I was able to play rock guitar, after a fashion. I bought instructional books. I experimented. I was the proud composer of "Cloudburst."

The band took the same name. It consisted of myself on guitar and occasional vocals, classmate Wendy Corn on vocals and guitar, and a rambunctious drummer. But I had no amplifier, and carting around my bulky stereo system was not practical. Wendy's friend Andrew, a tech whiz kid whom she would later marry, rewired some contraption so that it functioned as a guitar amp. And a classmate known for his deep pockets invested in a portable light show.

Cloudburst performed at a few parties. I dimly recall our drummer starting a fight. And I remember a sense of heady euphoria while strumming and singing "Brown Sugar" at one basement party.

I also have fond memories of playing guitar and singing in my own basement, a microphone hanging from one of the lantern light fixtures that dangled from the ceiling. On one occasion when my parents were out of town, I did my best to impress a female classmate with vodka, orange juice, and an original song. I still recall some of the lyrics: *I've been flying on the ocean / swimming on the moon / and I'm still in love with you / if I change my mind tomorrow / I hope you change your mind too.*

Music had become a key part of my young life. At fourteen I crafted a homemade passport on lined paper, complete with photograph, signature, height, weight, bank, brand of skates, and "Occupation: GUITARIST." A couple of years later, on a green blotter that sat on a desk where I was meant to do homework, I inscribed a sort of mission statement to myself in red ink: "Music is my outlet of frustration / My shelter of sadness / My expression of happiness / My tool of originality and creativity / The cause of my enjoyment / And my recess in an otherwise restricted and compulsory day." That summed up the situation pretty neatly, if sophomorically.

I purchased a higher-quality guitar, a maple-bodied Gibson L6, which has remained my sole electric guitar to this day. I also befriended Keith McKenna, a musician who tinkered on several instruments, and together we started a band called Wet Paint. The band got its name on the night of our first gig, when we found a sign left by painters and placed it in front of the kick drum. Wet Paint performed a bunch of thinly attended club shows and recorded a handful of original songs on a friend's four-track reel-to-reel recording machine. The chorus for one of the songs, which really felt as if it was bound to be a hit, declared that the singer was *looking for my end of the rainbow* and that it *better happen before I get too old.*

Was I really trying to "make it"? I don't believe I ever had the notion that this was possible. There were certainly some high points, such as performing at a downtown street festival and recording on that four-track machine. I even had a meeting alongside my bandmate McKenna with a Sony Music executive, playing him two songs on a cassette we'd recorded. His reaction wasn't bad, a come-back-when-you're-better kind of thing.

University and then journalism took over my life, while songwriting remained a hobby. By that time, my musical tastes had meandered away from the Stones in the direction of Dire Straits, Elvis Costello, and J. J. Cale, as well as jazz and "world beat" artists, usually guitar-oriented. I put my Gibson L6 in the closet as if it were a thing of adolescent exuberance, grew a beard, and played only my Harmony archtop acoustic guitar. From time to time there were bursts of activity. I joined forces with a supremely talented vocalist I met at Concordia University named Rebecca Campbell, who would go on to front many bands. And later, while studying history, I teamed up with Michael Leon, a class-mate who was a gifted multi-instrumentalist. We played in a band that recorded songs on a friend's eight-track machine, performed once at a raucous loft party, and dissolved after Leon left town.

In the late 1990s, I switched jobs at the Montreal *Gazette* from covering general news to being the pop music critic. It was a one-year gig, but it refreshed the playlist in my head. And then I discovered Johann Sebastian Bach. Along the way, I never gave up on playing guitar. The desire to write songs never went away.

MANSION ON THE HILL

CARRYING A GUITAR IN public has always produced a visceral pleasure for me. The sensation, lodged in my teenage brain, comes from an aura of cool conferred by the instrument. On this particular occasion, a Taylor acoustic was slung over my shoulder in its black nylon case as I approached Morey Richman's home.

I knew Morey from when we were students together at Vanier College, which was housed in a drab office building overlooking the Decarie Expressway in Montreal. We played guitar together once. I never got to know him well, recalled only that his fretboard skills were formidable.

A generation later, I bumped into him in the Starbucks on Sherbrooke Street where I'd met Jo that same month. Despite the passage of decades — his once-wavy mop of hair had thinned and receded — I had easily recognized him at the café. He is short and compact, giving the impression of coiled strength. His pale blue eyes, the colour of a swimming pool, have an intensity that borders on combativeness. His heavy five o'clock shadow was many hours ahead of schedule.

"Still playing guitar?" he asked.

"Never stopped. You?"

"Oh yeah. Still writing?"

"Yep."

"I used to read your stuff when you wrote about music for the *Gazette*," Morey said.

"The job had its charms. But I can't say I miss doing that anymore," I said. "What line of work are you in?"

"I'm retired."

"Retired?" Morey couldn't have been much older than fifty.

"Yeah, I played in touring bands for many years, then I started a record company. Eventually I sold it."

"Wow."

I told Morey about my desire to record original songs. We exchanged email addresses and now, a few emails later, I was standing outside his home in the affluent, tree-studded neighbourhood of Upper Westmount. The greystone mansion, located after some difficulty, towered fortress-like over the street as if built to withstand a siege. Guitar in hand, I climbed several flights of vertiginous stairs and rang the doorbell.

Morey beckoned me inside.

"You didn't have to bring that," he said, gesturing toward my guitar.

I followed him two floors up and entered what he called his "lab" — a vast A-frame attic. Scattered here and there were half a dozen guitar stands, each holding three guitars upright, some electric, some acoustic, some archtop jazz models, sculptural displays of string and wood scattered across the big room, beautiful specimens all. My steel-string Taylor, however cool it made me feel en route, should have stayed at home.

The renovated attic also contained a television, a couple of guitar amplifiers, some microphones, and shelves of CDs. Oriental throw rugs lent some colour to a wood floor salvaged from a barn. And at the centre of the room was a small desk of dark wood with a laptop sitting on it—what passes for a sound recording studio in the early twenty-first century.

We sat down on a tan leather couch and began swapping life stories. Morey started from the beginning: he'd grown up in a gritty district of central Montreal until his parents scraped together enough money to buy a modest home in Côte-Saint-Luc, a west-end neighbourhood. "My father worked in the garment business—he was a dress cutter," Morey told me. His mom did some bookkeeping.

"How was it that you started playing guitar?"

"I don't know," he said. "I remember bugging my parents to get me a guitar for a while. At nine they caved and got me one of those crappy Stella little things with the strings nine feet above the neck. They made me take lessons with some old man who was a taxi driver. He made me learn 'Baa Baa Black Sheep,' and I hated it. I wanted to play like Eric Clapton. But I never practiced; I pretended to. I used to move the pages of the book so they'd think I'd been practising."

Not surprisingly, he quit some time afterwards.

"And how did you get back into it?"

Morey said that a couple of years later he took it up again at a summer camp singalong. "You know, sitting around the campfire, James Taylor songs, and everyone gathers around you and you get attention: wow—the cool kid playing guitar! Then I got really into it; I wanted an electric guitar."

Morey's father—who himself occasionally picked up an old guitar and also played a bit of harmonica—reluctantly agreed to buy his son an electric guitar. The eye-popping result, purchased at a second-hand shop in Old Montreal, was a white double-necked Mann.

Thus equipped, Morey started to master the progressive rock material—Genesis, Yes, Gentle Giant—that was dominating turntables in Montreal at the time. He told me he got together with a drummer and "a little kid who played a monster organ." A bassist joined, and a band was born. "That started the whole thing."

His band was called Labyrinth, and its high point was a school concert that went over big with the student audience. After high school, he continued to apply himself to guitar and jammed with various people (myself included, when we met at Vanier). He enrolled in a music engineering institute but dropped out. He then tried creative writing at Concordia University (where I was also studying, though we never crossed paths), but he was "half-assed" about it and only really wanted to play in a band. Tension at home boiled over when he quit university.

"My parents weren't going to support me. I was unwelcome with my current status," he said. "I left the house, crashed with a friend in [the neighbourhood of] NDG, had odd jobs—cutting grass in a cemetery, lugging supplies at McGill University—and roamed from band to band. I wanted to be a session musician. I was into all those guys in L.A. who used to do all the sessions. And that's what I wanted to be. But I joined a few bands, played here and there, made a few dollars. I didn't really want to play live; I was always kind of nervous. I didn't think I looked good enough, moved well enough, I wasn't the rock star type. But I wanted to play, so finding a band to play in was the only way I could make a little bit of money and maybe record with the guys I was playing with."

From the age of about twenty-one, he started playing in a bunch of groups, ranging from a Police tribute band to a group called Isinglass, formed by ex-members of the successful new wave act Men Without Hats.

Morey had no shortage of stories from his gigging life. He told me that once, after a show in a small town in northern Quebec, a woman who claimed to be at risk from an abusive husband asked him whether she could sleep in his hotel room. There was no sex involved; he was being a good guy. "Sure enough, the next morning I woke up and all my stuff was gone. Like, everything was gone: my guitar, the money I was making, my clothes, everything. That was quite a little lesson in rock 'n' roll."

Morey kept asking me questions about the career of a journalist, but I wanted to know how a rock guitarist had made it up the hill to a Westmount mansion. "So you were in your twenties playing in different bands. What happened next?" I asked.

"I got wind of a band that was already touring and was looking for a guitar player," he said. "I took a bus up to Quebec City [for the audition]. I didn't speak French very well, but I figured I'd go anyway. I made the band. They were already known and were pretty established. We went all over Quebec, many, many times—everywhere. The band was called the Game. We made demo tapes. We were interviewed on CHOM radio. We really thought we were about to make it. But nothing happened."

"Nothing?"

"Nothing."

At its peak, the Game, which specialized in Top 40 songs by the likes of Queen, U2, and Pink Floyd, included a sound man, a light man, and a separate truck contracted to ship their gear to every gig. Morey was constantly in a van on the road; sleeping arrangements left much to be desired.

"The first two years were a lot of fun, then after that it was like, oh, Baie-Comeau again! The people don't get any older in the clubs, they're still eighteen, nineteen, and you're now twenty-three, and then you're twenty-four, twenty-five. It becomes a little bit of a grind at that point, but you need to do it because you need the money and the band wants to make it and you're writing songs and trying to get that going."

The rock life didn't seem to be adding up to anything with a future.

"I had given myself until the age of thirty to make it, so to speak, or at least to have some inkling of advancement," Morey said. "And when I got close to thirty and I was still touring the same clubs and we hadn't gotten anywhere with our original stuff, I decided that at thirty I would leave."

He found work at a record store chain, Discus, trading the stages of rock clubs for a tiny kiosk in a downtown Montreal mall. "I was thirty years old," he told me, "working in a record store for minimum wage and sleeping on a friend's couch. I was totally depressed—thirty years old with nothing, no education, no skills. And I was also playing in a Portuguese wedding band on the side."

But his musical smarts were noticed at Discus, then the country's biggest record store chain, with 120 outlets. He was soon doing data entry, albeit for minimum wage, at the company's head office in the Montreal suburb of Saint-Laurent. When the head music buyer suffered a nervous breakdown, the position needed to be filled quickly and Morey volunteered to step in. The post became permanent. He spent his days determining how many CDs of bands like Genesis, Metallica, and the Eagles would go to what stores. He brought to the job a touring musician's knowledge of what was likely to be popular. His picks sold well.

One importer, however, was peeved that Morey wasn't buying bargain CDs from his parent company in Holland. From Morey's vantage point, the product was too European, not sufficiently tailored for the North American market. The British importer took Morey out for dinner one night, complained bitterly, and later made a surprising offer: come into business with me.

Morey explained to me a complicated chain of events that followed. He joined the Canadian branch of the Dutch company, which soon ran into trouble and was bought by three individuals, including the British importer; the new owners then sold the company to an American conglomerate, which in turn tanked. The upshot was that Morey and the British importer created a new record company "on the ashes of the old one." His British partner, who had an entrepreneurial background and raced cars as a hobby, became the president of the new company. Morey became the vice-president, in charge of music content. They named their new company the St. Clair Entertainment Group.

St. Clair specialized in buying or licensing master tapes

that could be creatively packaged as budget or compilation CDs. Morey recalled his first move as if it had happened the previous day: he purchased one hundred hours of inexpensive classical music from a European conductor who'd secured the rights to music played by no-name orchestras and obscure soloists. Morey re-packaged those one hundred hours into several hundred hours of CDs. He "dumbed it down" with collections like *Piano Music on a Sunday Afternoon*, *Classics for Kids*, and *Classical Music from the Movies*.

"It went crazy—people loved it," Morey said, picking up his tempo and speaking with his hands, as if the guitarist in him never quite disappeared. "Not many companies were doing it. We tried to open that up and do it in a bigger way. Rather than try to sell the cheapest stuff possible, the shlockiest junk, a lot of our stuff was licensed from major independent companies that we would compile so that it appealed to a lot of people... But we actually tried to sell the idea that, for example, here are the best blues guitar players, the B. B. Kings, the real stuff, but our price point was impulse buy."

Morey pulled a number of CDs off his shelf to illustrate some of St. Clair's productions. There was a series called *A Celebration of Blues*, which was followed up with similar collections for jazz, reggae, and Celtic music. The company's offerings were very much a mixed bag: recordings of B. B. King, Charlie Parker, and the Kinks alongside New Age music geared for yoga, Halloween Sounds, and demo tapes Santana recorded before he became famous.

Morey said his label made inroads in what at the time were unconventional retail places for music—big box stores like Costco, Best Buy, and Walmart; airport shops, coffee shop chains, even lingerie stores. The old-school record company execs, Morey said, couldn't be bothered to market unconventional products in these unconventional places. The big recording companies were focused on finding the Next Big Thing. A minuscule proportion of acts in fact "made it," but that's how the business worked. Instead, Morey looked elsewhere for music, whether commissioning an accordion virtuoso or snapping up the rights to recordings rock bands made between contracts.

"Our idea was to take valuablé older catalogue, recompile it, make it kind of new again at a lower price for an impulse-buy decision in a non-traditional market. Just renew the whole thing. And the major companies weren't doing that."

"Not as glamorous as signing the next Nirvana," I said.

"It was very unglamorous," he said. "But it paid the bills."

I kept stealing glances at the array of fine guitars in the attic studio. I was itching to pick one of them up. "And your guitar playing?"

Morey said that after his touring life came to an end, he stopped playing guitar altogether. But that changed, he recounted, at a barbecue in the American Midwest, hosted by a Walmart executive. The exec owned an old guitar signed by a ton of rock stars. Someone mentioned over dinner that Morey used to play. He was asked to give it a whirl and he did, strumming and picking his way through a hootenanny of singalong tunes, beginning with John Cougar Mellencamp's "Jack & Diane." "Everyone loved it," Morey said. Business with Walmart picked up and took off. It was the most lucrative gig he ever played.

In a few short years, Morey had gone from couch surfing,

earning minimum wage, and playing in a Portuguese wedding band, to running a record company that was shipping up to forty million units a year. The office was in suburban Saint-Laurent, employing as many as sixty people. Morey and his partner, Jill, bought a home; a daughter, Hayley, was born, then a son, Jarrett.

Yet, despite the success, Morey felt out of sync with his new life. "I was kind of dragged into the business thing," he told me. "I was a guitarist. It wasn't really me."

Morey's timing as an entrepreneur had been impeccable. The decade from 1990 to 2000 saw high profits in the music business as CDs replaced vinyl collections. The year 1999 represented the peak year in annual sales. But that same year featured "mp3" as the most popular search term on the Internet; with file-sharing sites like Napster on the rise, record-industry sales would plunge from that point on.

"I was feeling the grind," he recalled. "I never felt that comfortable as a nine-to-fiver. We all could smell the way the industry was going with file-sharing. And the major record companies were starting to capitalize on the success that companies like us had; they made it much harder for us to get licensing material because they wanted to do it. Prices of CDs kept coming down; all of a sudden you could walk into any Walmart and there was a bin of, like, Aerosmith at the same price that we were selling two hundred classical favourites. All the profits that we were making were going back into new inventory . . . It became sort of like touring the clubs. I wanted to get off the hamster wheel. It started getting to me. It was stressful. I wanted to sell."

Finally, in 2003, Morey and his partner sold their record company for a princely sum to a New York–based private equity firm that owned, among many other holdings, a boat manufacturer and a hair salon franchise. A few years later there was a sad epilogue: the record label went bankrupt.

That brought his story more or less up to the present. Morey walked over to one of the many guitar stands in his studio and selected an elegant acoustic, handing it to me. He took another instrument that had been handcrafted to his taste. We started jamming. I ran through my original songs and he played along, sounding divine every step of the way. He laced all my songs with expert funk, rock, or jazz licks. Midas Richman on the fretboard.

Morey's musical energies were focused on recording cover versions of pop songs with his thirteen-year-old daughter, Hayley. In the process, he was teaching himself how to record in state-of-the-art fashion, using computer software to conjure up any sound under the sun. Aside from his high-calibre guitar playing and his daughter's voice, all the instruments were computer-generated sounds. To weave everything together required a very good musical mind, all the skills of a producer and arranger, albeit one working with a laptop, not live musicians.

It began as a father-daughter bonding thing, with Morey determined to bolster Hayley's confidence and keep her away from questionable social influences. Yet it quickly became apparent that Hayley possessed an exquisite voice. The videos of Hayley singing songs by Adele, Christina Aguilera, Coldplay, Fleetwood Mac, Leonard Cohen, and U2, in the lush soundscapes that Morey was creating, were posted on YouTube. A teenage dream come true.

Meanwhile, my own arrested adolescent fantasy was unfolding.

SONG CASTLES IN THE SAND

THE MAIN REASON I'D gotten in touch with Morey after we'd bumped into each other was that I'd decided to record my songs. Since the days of Cloudburst, I'd played in a handful of bands. From time to time there had been fitful attempts at recording on rudimentary equipment. Now, a few decades into the songwriting process, I felt ready to make a truly professional recording. A dozen songs struck me as fully composed. What had long been a hobby had become an obsession.

My plan was to press various musician friends into service. And Morey had suddenly become the highest-calibre musician I knew.

A couple of weeks after our first jam, Morey swung by my place to play music again. A pipe in my bathroom had sprung a leak earlier in the day, but we kept on jamming while a plumber worked on the situation. We went through a dozen of my songs, all embroidered by Morey's golden touch. A highlight for me was jamming on the song "Battlefield Mind." Morey's intricate counter-melody line brought the tune to a gloriously jazzified new level.

"Battlefield Mind" was an apt symbol for my reinvigorated songwriting. It had been composed a few years earlier. After working as a rock critic for the Montreal *Gazette*, I chanced upon a performance of J. S. Bach's *Cello Suites*, a hypnotic sequence of music that rewired my audio circuitry and set me on a seven-year journey of discovery. I focused exclusively on classical music during that search, a refreshing development after overdosing on Top 40 as a music critic.

When that journey culminated with the publication of a book about Bach, I was suddenly free again to listen to whatever turned my crank, classical or not. I rediscovered the joys of James Brown, Bob Dylan, Radiohead, and Massive Attack. Letting my hair down further, I dusted off my old electric guitar, plugged it into an amp, and out came a song so simple in design, so primitive and raw, that it was best understood as a rocking-out release from the sedate, highbrow atmosphere that had delighted but also circumscribed seven years of my life.

"Battlefield Mind" started with the most basic of chords, an A major, played in the simple open position, moving to a repetitive hammering a few frets higher up the fingerboard. This simple riff was combined with a high, lonesome vocal melody that would not have been out of place in the Appalachians. I even tried recording it on my laptop's GarageBand software. I threw in a scorching guitar solo that surprised me with its distorted ferocity.

It was initially titled "Friendly Fire" and featured some

fuzzy lyrics about *floating on a mushroom cloud / watercolour grey / soft power fading now / showing my age.* I sang it as best I could. Which is to say not terribly well. But the result had a Woodstockian charm. ("Groovy," was Jo's reaction. "Makes me want to drop acid!")

It was clear that without fleshed-out instrumentation, without bass or drums and perhaps other instruments, it would never come into its own as a song anyone would want to listen to. But Morey's guitar playing had squeezed upscale harmonies out of the rawness, ennobling what in my hands was a primitive rock song.

I asked Morey if he had any critique of my songs, whether some worked better than others.

"No," he replied, "they all work just fine, except maybe that last one." He was talking about "Grace of Love," for which he imagined a massive anthemic buildup, U2-style, taking the pre-chorus in double time. We tried to do it, in vain. It was clear the big idea was locked up inside his head.

"I'd have to record it," he said. "But," he added by way of a warning, "it might end up sounding very different."

The idea of a straight singer-songwriter version of my songs—that is to say, the way I played them, the only way they really could be played solo—didn't grab Morey. His approach to song production was to go big, mix as many elements as possible in the test tubes of his laptop studio, and remix till he was satisfied.

Ironically, the song of mine that seemed to work least well for him was the one he was most interested in. Perhaps precisely because it was a fixer-upper and he could carry out his own renovations.

I was somewhat worried that we didn't have quite the

same musical tastes. He was never into the Rolling Stones, the Who, or the Grateful Dead, all formative influences when I was a teenager. His musical role models were guitarists like Eric Clapton, Jimmy Page, and Buddy Guy, to be followed by progressive rock bands like Yes, and later on fusion jazz guitarists. I imagined that "Grace of Love" in Morey's hands would bear no resemblance to the song I'd composed.

After our jam, I kept trying to improve the pre-chorus and the chorus, the parts that he had anthemic ambitions for. I had a guitar-driven hook with a melody over it that formed a nice verse; that much I was sure of. It very nearly stood on its own, but would in all likelihood get droningly repetitive. So it needed to go somewhere, and that was where the uncertainty and anguish lay. When a fully formed song magically arises in your head, rare though that occasion may be, it is easy. When you try to expand on a rough idea to make a complete song, it is hard. Clichés lie in wait. You may cobble together something that is overly folkie, predictably rocking, or pompously jazzy. Resemblances to famous songs threaten your every move.

I thought I'd finally finished "Grace," but once again, unsettled by Morey's critique, I was left with half a song.

IT WAS GOOD weather for melancholic songs that needed completion. December had the city in cold storage. Citizens were subjected to all the downsides of winter — dirty snow hugging the edges of sidewalks, black ice, howling cold, gunmetal skies — and none of the perks of the season; no cotton-batting fluffy snow, no snow-coney confetti showers, no brilliant sun illuminating the freshly ironed sheets of whiteness.

I was in the songwriting trenches when I received a text from Jo about a struggle of her own.

J: Working on a new riff. It's driving me crazy. I really need to get all these songs recorded.

E: Know the feeling. I've been anguishing over "Cherries" this AM. Trying to remember one change I made to the chorus ages ago. And I hyperventilate when I sing it.

J: Send me what u have — haven't heard it for a while.

"Cherries" was written for my grandfather. I had made an improvement to the chorus earlier in the year and was having trouble remembering it. I rummaged through old iPhone recordings I'd made on the fly. Nothing turned up. So I worked it out, guesstimating as best I could what the change would have been.

The song had a sparseness, a minimalism, a meditative quality that captured my deep affection for my grandfather, who was born in 1914 in the east end of Montreal. Although the lyrics may suggest cherry blossoms in all their ethereal and explosive glory, the roots of the song were more ordinary. When my grandfather was ailing, I'd ask him if there was anything I could bring him on my next visit. "Cherry Blossom," was his usual reply — the chocolate bar that his wife had deemed too unhealthy for an ailing octogenarian.

"Old age," he would say, "is not for sissies."

I'd smuggle the Cherry Blossom into his apartment.

Jo had always liked the song. I tried to record its latest incarnation for her on the iPhone, but I kept flubbing it. After some time I was finally getting it right, and then the phone rang in the middle of the second verse. I didn't have another take in me. I emailed it, untimely phone call and all.

E: Sent you 60 seconds of the thing.

J: K.

Pause.

J: Very pretty. Too bad was abridged version.

E: Thanks. Does chorus work for you?

J: Yup.

That was the best word I'd read all week.

E: How's your riff?

J: Riff is stiff. Can't seem to evolve past it.

E: Normally a riff is all you require.

J: What r u implying sir?

This touched a nerve. I often recommended that Jo tone down her riffs so that they are not overexposed in her songs.

She liked to dwell on one riff and let her flowing vocal melodies work their magic.

> E: *That you're so talented that a riff is usually foundation enough for you to build an impressive song castle.*

> J: *Sometimes a gal needs a little bricks n' mortar for her musical fortress.*

Later, I checked in on her.

> E: *Any riff progress? Need help from the riff repairman?*

> J: *It's over. I realized I was writing "Imagine" by Lennon. I think the well had run dry. Now I'm wondering how many of my songs are actually riff-offs.*

BASEMENT SESSION NO. 1

WHEN I TOLD MOREY that I wanted to record my songs, he offered to get in touch with an old high school bandmate of his, a drummer who plays in a wedding band, makes instructional videos about sound recording, and has a small studio in his home. He would come cheaper than a big commercial studio.

A week after our jam at my place, Morey emailed to say that he'd spoken to his friend "with the little home studio, and he says he'd record whatever you want, live drums (he would play them if you'd want), do all engineering, etc., for forty-five dollars an hour. Rest assured that I can vouch for his work. He is not only a first-rate musician (drums especially but is also very capable on keyboards) but an extremely competent recording engineer as well. He would use software and computers for recording, mixing, mastering, etc."

I exchanged emails with Eli Krantzberg and we set up a meeting at his home, located on a tree-lined residential street near Concordia University's Loyola campus, at the far western end of the city. The holiday season was approaching, and the modest home had its spiritual bases covered, with a window display of little red Santas as well as a Jewish mezuzah affixed to the door frame.

"I know you from somewhere," Krantzberg said in greeting. He was a small, trim man with a kindly face, receding hairline, and long sideburns speckled with grey. He introduced me to his fiancée, Mariam, who emerged from the small kitchen.

When told of the Morey connection, she mused about how successful their high school band Labyrinth had apparently been. "They even had groupies," she said, arching an eyebrow. "Did you know that?" Krantzberg cracked a smile and seemed to relish the memory.

Leaving Mariam upstairs, we descended to the basement studio, passing framed photographs of jazz greats and some cheesy publicity shots of the various hotel and wedding bands he'd played in over the years.

There was not much in his "studio," aside from a computer monitor on a very neat desk and a small mixing console. At one side of the room, sectioned off with baffles, was a set of blond wood drums and several microphones on stands leaning in at various angles. The dimensions of the room were Lilliputian, with exposed water pipes running overhead at a height well below six feet. An upright bass would have trouble fitting.

Krantzberg explained how the computer-based recording process would work. He was affable and efficient. One look at how neat his desk was, how organized his recording system appeared, and I knew I would never tumble into the technological rabbit hole that comes with so many home studios. I remembered my own ill-fated attempts at home recordings with friends from long ago, forever searching for the root of some fugitive buzz or mysterious glitch.

"No time will be lost to tech issues," Krantzberg said. I didn't doubt him. But I feared that my rock 'n' roll adventure in such an antiseptic environment would feel about as adventurous as cutting a record in my dentist's office. Yet Krantzberg was undoubtedly a good guy, not one to throw any curveballs, and inspired complete confidence. His rate was cheaper than a big studio's, and this was as good a place as any to see whether my songs might amount to anything. I told him I'd mull things over and get back to him.

The following week, I emailed him my green light and we scheduled a first session for a Thursday afternoon.

The session coincided with the first major snowstorm of the season. I took a cab to Krantzberg's home, passing daredevil kids snowboarding on the streets and a city bus beached on a snowbank like a dying whale. I wanted to partake in what was shaping up as the most spectacular snowstorm in decades. But at two o'clock I clomped across the snowed-in walkway to Eli Krantzberg's bungalow and disappeared into the preternatural quiet of the basement studio.

As I pulled my guitar out of its hard-shell case I noticed Aristotle and Plato on the bookshelf beside the drum kit. I asked Krantzberg about the books, and he told me he went back to university when he was in his mid-twenties to study political science. He offered me Christmassy drinks, we discussed his new cellphone, which he'd nicknamed "the Man," and then we got down to business.

"So what's the name of the song we're going to do?" Krantzberg asked.

"Basement Rainbow."

I occupied a high-backed chair and picked up my guitar, and Krantzberg gave me a pair of headphones. He set up a stand with a microphone pointed to my guitar's soundhole. I tuned up and could hear every nuance amplified through the headphones. It sounded sweet. After spending so much time recording myself on my iPhone, it felt luxurious to have someone else at the controls.

I had decided to start with "Basement Rainbow" because I thought it was one of my better compositions and an easy one to play. It's a slow, folkie song that chronicles a few encounters compressed into one narrative. It has a catchy little guitar hook at the start that I return to after every chorus.

"I like it," Morey had emailed after I sent him an iPhone recording of Jo singing it with me on guitar. "I can see this song either taking shape as a singer/songwriter type thing (like it is now) or fully fleshed out with an electric Wallflowers/Counting Crows–type vibe."

Jo had helped me immeasurably with the song simply by suggesting I ditch its previous chorus and use what was then the song's bridge as a chorus. I was initially reluctant to scrap a chorus that seemed to work fine with the words "Everything was shimmering in the greater scheme of things."

"I like that chorus," I told Jo.

"Use it for some other song," she said.

As was so often the case, her instincts were dead on. "Greater Scheme of Things" thus became "Basement Rainbow." The result was less of a rambling countrified number and more of a tender ballad.

But I was mistaken in thinking any song would be easy to record. For starters, what's known as a "click track" was rubbing me the wrong way. This was essentially an electronic metronome that Krantzberg was piping into my headphones with the correct tempo, designed to keep a performer in perfect time. It's pretty standard in the world of recording, though many are vehemently opposed to it. Some musicians prefer to weave in and out of perfect time, going with the organic flow of live performance. They may want to deliberately change tempo, speed up, or slow down for effect. But in contemporary recording, especially if you want to "overdub" other instruments down the road, a click track provides a sturdy foundation that can be safely built upon.

The click, however, felt unsettling to me, as if I were being placed in rhythmic handcuffs. I requested a change in the tone of the click, from chirpy to something with more bass. Krantzberg obliged. The tightness of the headphone cord was annoying my back and arm. Krantzberg produced an extension cord. It then dawned on me that playing the tune on guitar without singing the words threw me off. Krantzberg was patient.

My mind wandered to the snow I was missing. It took me a while to get the guitar track down, and when I did I wasn't convinced of the performance. The lead vocal track went okay, it seemed, but when we played it back, some of the choruses were better than others. Krantzberg was able to digitally graft the good choruses onto places where bad performances had previously been. It felt a bit dishonest.

Next I started on "Country Mile," a more straightforward tune bordering on country rock. This was, in a way, the song that launched the whole project. It took me a very long time to come up with a chorus that did justice to the verse. The words were fairly easy to come by, written in the aftermath of my breakup with Nathalie. Love and death may be the two main wellsprings for composition, and breakups combine the two themes.

The song progressed nicely, though once or twice I thought of Nathalie, and at one point made an error while hearing in my head a line from the last verse: *miss you and I always will*. I imagined her strolling snowy Mont Royal atop the city, delighting in the pristine white blanket. Then I forced myself to focus and sang the song decently.

When I took a seat next to Krantzberg to listen to the take, I felt drained and buried my face in my hands, poised to listen and hope for the best. He misinterpreted my body language.

"Is she married now?" he asked.

"Maybe."

"I had one of those too."

Perhaps he was right. The song was a lament, and quite possibly I was still feeling it.

Three hours had disappeared by then. It was costing me. I needed some air. And I wanted to catch the raging shutdown of civilization. I left my guitar in Krantzberg's basement and ventured out into a world transformed.

With the sidewalks buried, the walk home took a very long time. Everywhere, people were wielding shovels, digging cars out of snowbanks as if they were on rescue missions in a white desert. Pedestrians trudged through the fluffy snow — fluffy, yet not benign; there was just too much of it.

The click track was now so much white noise. The snowstorm, the heaviest in nearly half a century, shut out the din from my head, the clamour of my own songs. It had not been a very successful session, and I welcomed the muffle and mute produced by fifty centimetres of snow.

BASEMENT SESSION NO. 2

THE NEXT DAY, I put on my cross-country skis and went about forgetting the music in my head. I skied over front yards and snowbanks and parks and city streets and alleged sidewalks. For all I knew I traversed buried automobiles as I made my merry way to Mont Royal — "the mountain," as it's known, that crowns Montreal.

The snow was mountainous manna, sublime in the extreme. Those who crossed paths on skis exchanged *bonjours*. "Greetings, fellow dweller of paradise." There were no sharp edges in this snow, only undulations. A landscape of soft landings.

As the snow settled over the city, I had several days to consider the "temp" (as in temporary) mixes of the two embryonic songs Krantzberg had emailed me after our session. I was impressed with how he was able to capture the full-bodied sound of my acoustic guitar. My singing was uneven, but that was a performance issue, no fault of the studio. "Country Mile" sounded serviceable; I would let it marinate until new instruments could be added to the mix. "Basement Rainbow" needed improvement. Meanwhile, I fine-tuned the arrangements for songs I'd try next time around.

A week after that first session, I was back in the basement studio, knowing better what to expect. The first song on my agenda was "Another Man's Crime." The tune, although a singer-songwriter thing in my hands, had propulsive groove. I thought it had soulful potential; I envisioned a horn section and sensual vocals. Even if it was several miles away from, say, Otis Redding, I could imagine Van Morrison doing it.

And mercifully it was not a breakup song. It was a murky story touching on identity theft and cybercrime. The words "stuck inside another man's crime" fit the chordplay in a way I could never shake. For me, writing a song involves stumbling upon some pleasing sequence of chords on guitar that I then try to sing over. The initial melody that comes to mind is like a mosaic pieced together with words. Usually you can improve those lyrics, but sometimes you're stuck with that initial pairing of words and music. One can only hope that the words filling the mosaic are more than just *maybe baby*. With "Another Man's Crime," opaque as the topic might have been, at least I had something other than heartbreak to work with. The first image that came to mind was that of a gunslinger seated at a computer.

Krantzberg and I determined the tempo — the beats per minute (BPMs). This is a crucial decision that (unlike nearly all other variables with computer-based recording) cannot be radically altered down the road. I took my seat on the high stool and strummed into a pair of Neumann mics with their heads positioned close together at a ninety-degree angle.

I laid down the guitar track without incident. Then, while listening to the guitar track on headphones, I sang the vocals.

Next up: I wanted to redeem myself with "Basement Rainbow." After the struggles of that first session, I realized that it was a song I had trouble singing if I wasn't playing guitar at the same time. My guitar playing needed my vocals, and vice versa.

I tried the simultaneous guitar/vocals approach and seemed to pull it off. The vocals were passable, maybe not good enough to make the final cut, but that would be on account of my dubious voice, not the actual performance. In any case, I hoped to get Jo to eventually sing the song.

"The microphone," reported Krantzberg, "is picking up too much sibilance."

"Sibilance?"

"It's basically *s* sounds, like a slight whistling noise. I'd like to try it again with a different microphone."

I was reluctant, as the imperfection seemed minor. He replaced the tube microphone, which happened to be his most valuable mic, worth $1,500, and we tried another take.

"I think I prefer that first mic after all," he concluded. Same sibilance issue. So we moved on. I wondered whether this was a sign his studio equipment was not up to scratch, but I suspected my vocal cords were the weak link in the technological chain.

That song behind me and as good as it was going to be for the moment, I took a crack at a newer composition called "Perfect Shell." The song has a quasi-country flavour, written on vacation while contemplating seashells in the harsh light of a relationship that seemed to be going nowhere.

Here I had difficulty doing vocals and guitar at the same time. The chorus, absurdly simple, nonetheless was tricky to sing; the lyrics don't float all that neatly over the chords. So I recorded the guitar and vocal parts separately.

I was in a productive zone. And this time I felt like I knew what I was doing. At one point Krantzberg swivelled around in his chair. He looked for all the world like Elvis Costello. "Why don't you try playing air guitar?" he said.

"Seriously?"

"Yeah, if you're used to singing while playing guitar. It's been known to work."

It initially felt ridiculous, and no doubt looked as much. But in fact it did help. I left Session No. 2 feeling as if I was on the right track.

The feeling, however, unravelled the next day, when Krantzberg emailed me the temp mixes. It was sobering. "Basement Rainbow," with vocals and guitar recorded in one fell swoop, sounded surprisingly good. But my vocals on "Perfect Shell" and "Another Man's Crime" were straining to stay in tune, as if those songs were in the wrong key for my voice. I couldn't say for certain whether the problems reflected underwhelming performances or were simply the product of an underwhelming voice. I had the right melodic shapes in my head but could not quite draw them out with my voice.

Remember when as a kid you first heard a newfangled device that recorded your voice and played it back? The shock of hearing one's own voice is off-putting for many people. An unkind mirror. That was the effect of Krantz-berg's temp mixes on me. I disliked the sound of my voice — vehemently disliked it.

INTERLUDE: TAKE ME HOME

A FTER THAT LAST SESSION with Krantzberg, I passed by Jimi's Music Store and made a mental note that I was overdue for a visit. Whereas my singing was a fraught issue, and songwriting could be excruciating, my guitar playing was respectable and the experience uncomplicated. To shape chords and noodle around the fretboard was pure pleasure.

There are very few guitar shops in town, but Jimi's, named after the string-bending divinity from Seattle, is one of them. I'd been meaning to replace a guitar that I'd given to a friend, a little country-and-western job, a three-quarter-size parlour guitar with a handsome pickguard and rosette. It was a looker and it felt good in my hands.

When my friend and I went our separate ways, I thought the guitar would be a meaningful keepsake for her. But I still missed the instrument and was aiming to find one that would be similarly easy to play. Maybe it would help me come up with a chorus for "Grace of Love."

I'd been recently charmed by a guitar at a big music store downtown; Seagull was the brand, made in Quebec. I fell for that guitar, but first I wanted to check out Jimi's because it usually has "seconds," B-stock guitars with superficial blemishes and knocked-down prices.

The Sherbrooke Street shop, sandwiched between a fish store and a money transfer joint, boasts a big speaker above its door, and as usual it was blasting passersby with monster guitar solos. I entered a small room crammed with merchandise, every inch of airspace filled with guitars dangling from ceiling pegs.

Eric, the owner, was at the cash in front. Jimi, his son, named after Hendrix, was in the back workshop fixing a guitar. Father and son, who look more like brothers, share a husky build and a rock 'n' roll irreverence. I asked Eric about Seagulls, and he located the same model I'd seen downtown; he grabbed it from a ceiling peg where it was hanging overhead with all the other instruments. As he reached for the guitar I noticed that his left hand was a gruesome sight. The flesh was peeling off his knuckles, and there was a general state of manglement that was probably putting a damper on his ability to play jazz chords.

"Whoa!" I said. "What happened there?"

"Ah, it's nothin'," said Eric, handing me the Seagull.

"Looks like *somethin'* to me. Fist fight?"

"Nah, some stupid thing. I was in the country at a bonfire and I was putting some lighter fluid on a big log when someone called my name, distracted me for a second, and that's all it took. The fire spread — like *fffwwwwttt!* — to my arms and legs. Good thing I was wearing a bathing suit."

I had trouble imagining him in a bathing suit.

"Anyway, even if my pants had caught fire, there was a lake nearby and I could've jumped in it."

The Seagull was in my hands by now, and I took a seat on a small wooden stool to see how it felt. I played a bunch of chords. Same guitar as in the big store downtown. Same model, same price, same look. Same everything, minus the magic. It did not whisper that same *take me home* in my ear.

In a way it was reassuring that model numbers and price points don't inexorably determine everything. Every guitar is carved from different pieces of wood originating from different trees rooted in different soils, battered by different storms and nibbled by different insects. Only so many guitars out there have my name on them.

"This is not doing it for me." I handed the Seagull Maritime sws Folk back to Eric. "What do you have that's one step up?"

"One step? It's a big step."

"Oh, yeah?"

"You'll have to pay another grand, more than another grand," he said. "That Seagull is better than guitars more expensive, until you get to about the $1,800 range."

"Really?"

"That's a fact."

"Well, what would be that next-step-up guitar?"

Eric surveyed the skyline of hanging instruments.

"Something like that Martin," he said, indicating a specimen that looked much like all the others in the fretboard forest. "Twenty-five hundred bucks."

"Twenty-five hundred?"

"Yeah. And it's second-hand."

"Can I give it a whirl? Just out of curiosity."

Eric tuned it up and couldn't resist showing off his bluesy chops. Then I took the Martin to a small wood stool beneath some gleaming electric guitars. Forget the Seagull. Forget any other guitar I'd ever played. This was the Holy six-string Grail. It boasted a Sitka spruce top, mahogany neck, intricate herringbone purfling and a matching rosette set against a deep sunburst.

A guitar, if there ever was one, that could finish "Grace of Love." Mind you, it wasn't easy to play. Heavy strings were set high off the neck, and I was doing digital calisthenics to form some big boxy chords on the first few frets. But the sound. The sound! One piddly D chord sent forth a rainbow of tones, undertones, and overtones. The whisper wasted no time in reaching my ears: *Take me home.*

I handed the guitar back to Eric.

"Sweet" was my verdict. "Wish you hadn't shown me that guitar."

"It's not called a Martin D-28 for no reason, you know what I mean," said Eric, referring to the iconic model number. "All those classic recordings from the sixties and seventies with acoustic guitar—most of them were played on a D-28. That's the sound in our head."

"Well, the sound in my head is now a bug in my ear," I told him. "I'll think about it."

"Save some pesos so you can buy it. What's it all for, anyway? Might as well enjoy it if you can."

He had a point.

"Take my buddy, Andy," he said, moseying over to the cash and warming to his theme. "He's dying, man—it's unbeliev-able. Younger than me. Went to the doctor for a regular checkup, and the doc sees this mark on his back. No big deal.

Andy's swarthy, see, he's Italian. Doc says, 'Well, if you wanna check it out you can get it checked out.' Andy goes home, and all he can hear is the doc's voice—*if you wanna check it out, check it out.* So he gets it checked out. Wham! They have to remove the thing. They take a chunk out of his back shaped like a diamond. Thick as a steak! So he's fine. Then earlier this year he finds some bumps under his arms. This time they don't even do a biopsy. Bang! They rip them all out. Don't even check them out. Put him on chemo and all that stuff. Andy! The guy's younger than me. And he hardly drinks, doesn't smoke. Unbelievable! Andy! It should be me, not him."

A thin guy with a neatly trimmed beard had been gingerly trying out an electric guitar. Now he was goggle-eyed, transfixed by Eric's tale. He ventured a comment.

"My dad," he said softly. "Same thing. Died of lung cancer. We were at a Passover Seder once. That's a Jewish—"

"I know what it is," said Eric.

"And there was a doctor there. My mom said, 'Why don't you ask him whether you should get it checked out.' The doctor said, 'Yes, you should get it checked out.' And that was it for my dad."

The three of us mortals, strangers, looked at each other with new-found intimacy and not a small measure of despair over the human condition, tempered by a fondness for steel strings affixed to pieces of wood. I felt compelled to add my own tale of woe.

"My father died when I was a kid. Heart attack."

By this time Eric had had enough bonding. His shop was a place of rock 'n' roll, not a twelve-step program.

"Moral of the story," he said, "save some pesos and buy the guitar."

BASEMENT SESSION NO. 3

KRANTZBERG WAS TELLING ME about a film he'd seen the night before called *Not Fade Away*. He was saying how he liked the movie's coming-of-age musical atmosphere, kids joining rock bands as a way out of the adolescent pressure cooker.

"And people like you stuck with it," I said.

It was difficult in a way to see Eli Krantzberg, the wedding-band drummer with his shiny black shoes and gingerbread bungalow, as an emblem of the 1960s. But why not? His drum playing and sound engineering skills were top-notch. And he'd managed to make a good living following his teenage fantasy—music.

As I followed him down to the basement studio, I couldn't help but notice a framed photo showing the drummer and his band in "ice cream suits"—all white, with pink shirts and white ties. They were called the Eli Krantzberg Trio, one of his many bands doing hotel gigs in the 1980s.

He eventually formed a seven-piece wedding band called Nightshift that still performs. But he had always cultivated an interest in the technology of music-making.

In the mid-1990s, Krantzberg enrolled in a sound recording course that focused on reel-to-reel machinery and what now seems like Stone Age editing methods — the use of razor blades to splice magnetic tape. Then he started learning the basics of what was emerging as a technological revolution in the history of sound recording: computer-based recording systems. The new technology was known as digital audio workstations, or DAWS.

DAWS did for sound "what the word processor did for the printed word," writes Greg Milner in *Perfecting Sound Forever*, a history of sound recording.

Sound recording has gone through many twists and turns since 1877, when Thomas Edison invented the acoustic phonograph. That enabled musicians to play into a metal horn that piped the sound into a glass diaphragm, which in turn vibrated to cut sound waves onto a soft wax master disc. Later came electrical recording, a similar system that converted those sound waves into electrical signals (via a microphone) that were etched into records. It greatly improved sound quality.

Yet recording engineers were still stuck with whatever sounds were originally recorded. The advent of magnetic tape in the late 1940s changed that, allowing for all manner of alterations by editing and splicing. And by the mid-1960s, multi-track recording on tape meant the individual parts of a song could be recorded separately, the music constructed layer by layer. Four-track recording systems became the norm, followed by eight-track recordings (such as the *White Album,* made by the Beatles in 1968), to be supplanted by sixteen-track, twenty-four-track, and forty-eight-track machines.

Then came digital, which makes recording infinitely changeable, faster, easier, and far less expensive. Home studios like Krantzberg's took off, while traditional high-end studios have been losing customers ever since.

"Digital recording," writes Mark Coleman in his book *Playback*, "turns the sound waves into a pulsating electric current that can be measured and expressed as a binary code of design." This means that sound is recorded directly onto a computer hard drive, manipulated in various ways with a mouse, and processed with "plug-ins" — software versions of real-life machines that provide sound effects like reverb, distortion, and compression.

DAWs such as Logic, Pro Tools, and Cubase became increasingly powerful and able to handle more and more plug-ins. Krantzberg was an early adopter of the DAW called Logic, which would eventually be purchased by Apple.

That was the technology story that led me to the basement studio. After discussing my plans for our third session, Krantzberg suggested we go to work on the drums first, explaining that once his girlfriend got back home it would be best not to make that sort of racket. (So much for the 1960s.)

I was concerned that his style of play might be too mechanical, too wedding-band for me. But to exclude his drums, when he's a drummer by vocation and his kit was set up and mic'd, would be impolite at best. I needed his goodwill. And it was worth a try.

He repaired to the nearby drum kit and its bookshelf lined with works by Foucault and Aristotle. He cued up the music for "Country Mile" and started playing drums

while listening to the tracks we'd recorded on headphones.
It didn't quite work for me. I requested a changed pattern
on the kick drum, a double kick instead of a single on the
second beat.

I left Krantzberg alone in that small drum space with
his Plato and *Intro to Political Theory,* so as not to stare. He
was a professional and could do this as easily, I suspected, at
Carnegie Hall as in his basement. He niftily controlled his
recording facility with a wireless keyboard by his side. After
one or two imperfect starts he quickly laid down a rhythm
and put aside his sticks. He went over to the computer and
looped and cut and pasted the thing. Next?

I was sitting beside him and contemplated creating a
bassline with the bass samples on his MIDI controller — a
keyboard used to play software sounds stored in the computer. He'd earlier assembled a bassline, but it hugged the
coastline of the progression too obviously and I disliked it.
Not his fault. I had tried the same with my own bass guitar
at home and it never worked. The song was so simple that
a bass just dutifully following the progression was overly
obvious. I got excited by the sounds of his software. But after
a minute or so I realized this was going to be a time-sucker
unlikely to produce a final bassline.

Instead, I wondered about piano. Krantzberg plays some
keyboards, and I had always imagined some simple piano
chords coming in on the chorus to give texture and lift. Tapping into the many sampled sounds at his digital fingertips,
we tried organ and electric piano, which did not fit as well
as acoustic piano. Krantzberg laid down a basic piano part
for the chorus, just forming the chords, nothing fancy. I
liked it very much.

I was tempted to keep going and building and layering the tune so that it became a complete song, but prudence and a sense of the money-clock ticking got the better of me. So we moved on.

"How about some more drums?" I said. "For 'Another Man's Crime.'"

Again Krantzberg got on the saddle behind his kit and tried a few beats. These he hit on quickly in a way that sounded splendid. I suggested that the song's various sections required different emphases—hook, verse, pre-chorus, chorus, a triple punch on the crash cymbal to resolve the chorus, followed by a big drum fill to reignite the groove.

Again it was off-the-cuff, and the house-band drummer didn't lose any time, laying down something that was serviceable and which I would later study. Ringo K. executed some beautiful stuff on the fly.

Heavy lifting remained, i.e., my voice—the voice with melody, timbre, and sibilance issues. I'd gone over the most recent temp mixes Krantzberg emailed, and I'd singled out the vocal lines that were off-key or just plain bad and which I thought we could redo—just splice in, a fix job—so that the songs with me singing them would be passable enough to give to a real singer without being deal-breakers.

I had some micro fixes planned for the vocals on "Another Man's Crime." And I figured we'd "punch in" new vocals for the problem areas. But Krantzberg had another idea. "Let's re-sing the whole song," he said. "It will sound smoother."

I incorporated some new ideas based on all the struggles I'd experienced with the song, changing the chorus here and there, ditching some sibilant words, and making various other small improvements.

And then the crucial revision, one that had dawned on me two days earlier. The vocal chorus would consist of three lines instead of four—I would not sing the tag line of *It's all locked inside* over those last three punchy chords. I'd always imagined a horn section emphasizing that last line anyway, providing brassy exclamation marks. The idea seemed to bear fruit. "Another Man's Crime" was in the clink, awaiting bail by a horn section, a funky bassline, and a soulful singer.

The final song I wanted to improve was "Perfect Shell"— or, as Krantzberg had mistakenly titled it in his computer, "Perfect Shelf." If it was ever going to have pride of place on a shelf, it badly needed refurbishing. The vocals were of course a big part of the problem. Also, I was dissatisfied with one spot in the song. I asked Krantzberg whether he might cut and paste some chords—like a skin graft—to give me a couple more measures before the bridge kicked in. Nothin' to it, said the software whiz. And so we digitally moved a bit of chordal skin from the song's posterior to its shoulder. It worked. A perfect shell game.

On to the vocal track. Once again we decided to have a go at the whole part. This seemed to improve the dossier. Except for the bridge, which, for a campfire-simple song, is somewhat complicated and stretches over no less than twelve chords. My first go at singing it was wonky. But it gave Krantzberg an idea that was interesting, if hurtful.

"Do you know what Auto-Tune is?" he asked.

I had heard of this controversial pitch-correction software, made famous by Cher on her 1998 chart-topper "Believe." I can't say I liked the notion. Auto-Tune is an audio processor that fixes vocals that are sharp or flat, like a spell-check for melodies. It has a dubious reputation for robotically repairing vocals that are off-key. Was I that bad?

"Let's just try it as an experiment," said Krantzberg. "It doesn't always work."

Rather than take umbrage, I agreed to the experiment. Perhaps Auto-Tuned I would be a singing sensation with no need for Jo or anyone else blessed with golden pipes.

Krantzberg opened the program and applied it to my rendition of the song's bridge. A graph of my vocals was plotted on the monitor. Angular horizontal lines dropped into little boxes and rose again into more boxes, like an EKG reading, though so angular as to suggest the vitals of a robot. Krantzberg showed me how all the little horizontal lines that were a bit sharp or flat would be automatically corrected when Auto-Tune was activated. It was like rounding off decimal points to form perfect whole numbers. We listened.

"Well," he concluded, "it doesn't always work."

That was clear. And I was glad for it. The idea that my vocals, wobbly as they might be, could be salvaged by a machine left me with a sinking feeling. I preferred to rise or fall on my own merits.

Whether it meant that I was too close to the mark or too far gone for Auto-Tune, I couldn't say. I wanted to think that I was all too human and my failings could thus only be alleviated by old-fashioned labour and luck.

The song was cued up again, and I resolved to sing that damn bridge and show the pitch-correcting software a thing or two. I finessed it on the first go-around. Pulled it off in overtime. The tune was happily placed on the Perfect Shelf.

By now Krantzberg's fiancée, Mariam, was back home, and we called it a day. He had a lot of things on his mind, in particular a new cellphone and provider that was giving him a lot of tech grief. This wizard of digital recording, this über-efficient software genius, was being flummoxed by the same cellphone headaches that plague us all.

I said goodbye to him and Mariam, who was in the kitchen hollowing out tomatoes that would be filled with bulgar and other ingredients. I praised the dinner-in-progress.

"He doesn't suffer," she said.

They were leaving in two days for Miami, where a Caribbean cruise awaited them. It was not Krantzberg's vacation fantasy; he'd never been on a cruise before, but the woman who kept him so well fed was enthusiastic. He was worried about how his new cellphone would fare. He had a lot of work messages to stay on top of during the upcoming days. After the cruise, he was off to Anaheim, where the National Association of Music Merchants annual show was being held. This was the world's biggest musical equipment and technology trade show.

"Lots of testosterone," said Mariam, rolling her eyes.

A COUPLE OF hours later, I received emails from Krantzberg with temp mixes of the three songs we'd recorded. Very pleasant indeed were the results. Nothing was perfect, but the drums added a lot, as did the little piano bits, and my vocals were decent. "Country Mile" had an easygoing likeability, and "Another Man's Crime," which I'd struggled with in recent weeks, seemed viable.

The early sessions had made me confront my own voice in the most unflattering play of light. Now I was having a heady, opposite experience.

That evening at a pizza joint, an old Top 40 hit reminded me of the nostalgic power of song. "My Sharona," by the Knack, has a propulsive drive, not unlike the much older tune by the Kinks, "You Really Got Me." I recalled being on a dance floor a long time ago and seeing a young woman in a black T-shirt emblazoned with *I ♥ New York*. I asked her to dance, and we ended up pleasantly entwined on a downtown bench. She has since become known as the Woman I Should Have Married.

At one point in our last session, Krantzberg asked me how long it had been since the breakup with the woman mentioned in my songs. The song we were listening to was "Another Man's Crime."

"This particular song is not about a woman," I said.

"Yes, but the other songs?"

About two years, I said. That was true of only one of the songs. "Perfect Shell" was about a year old and inspired by someone who asked me to bring her some seashells from a seaside vacation. "Basement Rainbow" is about no less than four people. The Woman I Should Have Married never got a song. "My Sharona" handles the memory.

Autobiographies can be DJ'd. A couple of slices later, the pizzeria sound system was piping "Who Can It Be Now?" I played that song in Wet Paint, my high school band, as a teenager with an outsized mop of black hair and a maple-bodied electric guitar.

After dinner, I went over to the NextDoor Pub, where local R&B sensation Shaharah was headlining her regular Thursday-night gig. The fabulous singer with magnetic stage presence engaged in her trademark air-fucking. Her backing trio was clicking with formidable bass-heavy precision. I thought of approaching her. For some time I'd imagined getting her to sing "Another Man's Crime." That would give it the aching soulfulness I'd been hoping for. But I shied away from talking to her after the set. Best to wait until I had a more complete version of the song that might interest her.

I walked home along Sherbrooke Street and couldn't resist playing "Another Man's Crime" on my iPhone, the version Krantzberg had emailed, holding the phone near my ear, alone on the unseasonably balmy winter sidewalk and grooving to the creation-in-progress. A creation scantily clad with instrumentation, true, but in my head it was fully fleshed out, showing off its curves and air-fucking the audience.

THAT WAS BEFORE the mercury sank like a silver stone and the housing stock became so many igloos where residents hunkered down to do anything, absolutely anything, indoors. Townhouse igloos, apartment block igloos, duplex igloos, mansion igloos—the whole frostbitten kit and kaboodle. Winter just would not be winter without the occasional malevolent reminder that life is full of suffering and we shouldn't get too big for our fur-lined boots. No snow, not much sun, and as one newscast lamented, "negative twenties." That's minus-twenty Celsius. Toss in the wind chill factor and it felt like negative thirties.

Cold enough for me to fetch my balaclava and start impersonating a burglar. The guy behind the counter at the fish store only half-worried when I burst into the shop, stamped my feet, clapped my lobster-claw gloves, and peered at him from behind the balaclava, which in turn was topped by an Afghan wool hat that covered my ears and left two braided woollen ponytails, like Hasidic strands of hair, dangling for no good functional or sartorial reason.

"What's fresh today?" I asked, doing my best to sound like I was not trying to hold up the joint. I left with cod, and later baked it and filled a frying pan with olive oil, onion, bok choy, cauliflower, oyster mushrooms, bell peppers, and tomatoes, all dusted with thyme and basil. I transported the heaping plate over to the TV and ate it while watching the Montreal Canadiens crush the Washington Capitals 4–1.

Giddy over the score, I decided to take my old Gibson electric guitar out of its battered case. I connected it to a small amplifier that I'd purchased in Florida as a teenager after winning at the dog races—the only time in my life I've ever been to the dog races, a sport that now fills me with puzzlement and disgust. But I had a little amp to show for it, a cube upholstered with the sort of grey flannel itchy material that dress pants were often made of when I was a kid and forced into wretchedly formal attire for some adult occasion.

It is not a great amp; one of the circuits is blown, one of the inputs has burn marks that resemble nicotine stains, and the result is far more distortion than I have any use for. But it was deliciously nostalgic to strap the heavy old Gibson L6 on my shoulder and play. I have had it since I was a teenager, the second electric guitar I ever owned, my one true amplified love.

FROM THE SKY

I WOKE UP EARLY and after toast and coffee grabbed the Gibson while frigid darkness governed the outside world. A song came into my hands. Just some unfamiliar chord shapes with rhythm, suggesting a melody of sorts, a melody that—it being so cold and dark and early—I sang in a low register. I had the notion that where I was going was more adventurous than usual, the sort of song that a younger person schooled on Radiohead might attempt. The thing seemed to take. And the electric guitar, as well as being easy on my fingers, was producing chords with a haunted intensity.

I remember Tori Amos playing a show I reviewed in Montreal and referring to ghosts lurking in the frozen underworld of the St. Lawrence River. At the time it struck me as amusingly eccentric. Now I was dredging up some ghostly presence of my own, gazing through my window at a besieged island city facing its Nordic enemy.

The song was written in the proverbial manner—as if from another hand. Or, given what would eventually be its title ("Honey from the Sky"), from somewhere high above. I have no idea how long the composition took to complete. Maybe the gist of it took about fifteen minutes. Tweaking took longer. And of course I could spend the next several years trying to get it right.

I got in touch with Jo because I knew she liked new material; she was always asking if I'd written anything new, which sort of made me feel like she had no fondness for anything I'd composed in the past. (It brought to mind an old journalism boss whose stock answer to any accomplishment was: "Yeah, but what have you done for me lately?") I emailed Jo the song, saying she might like it because I knew she had a thing for melancholic tunes. She replied: "And you like endless emotionless songs that talk about papyrus. So there, we're even. Will give a listen." The verdict: "Think you've got something there!"

Later she texted an afterthought: "Strange but every time I ride u for not being emotional enough I remind myself not to get too mired in my own feelings. I'm writing different now and I think it has a little to do w u. Very interesting time creatively for me. :)"

Within hours, the song was like a murky dream, recalled in the vaguest terms from a shadow world of consciousness. Was a song really written? I knew it had been; too much energy went into it to think otherwise. But had it not been recorded, jotted down first thing in the morning like a strange dream, I would not for the life of me be able to play it again.

RECENT DAYS HAD provided innumerable permutations of grey and general dreariness. My song project, two weeks after my last session with Krantzberg, felt like a waiting game on icy sidewalks with sooty snow and muck.

Desperate to record more songs, but with Krantzberg away cruising the Caribbean, I pinned my hopes on a meeting with one Howard Bilerman, whose name had kept popping up when I talked about recording to people in the know. I googled him, and he turned out to be a producer of note who works out of a renowned studio called Hotel2Tango. He replied to my query, but only offered me twenty-five minutes the next week. What was that? A dental appointment? Half a therapy session?

I also emailed a spunky singer I'd met in the Burgundy Lion pub a year back; we had jammed once in the park, and it seemed to go well. She ignored my email. And I crossed paths at the cinema with a professional violinist with whom I had discussed my music project not long ago; he was either in a rush, had poor eyesight, or deliberately blew me off. Morey, meanwhile, had not emailed me in more than a month, presumably unwilling to face me and say that "Grace of Love" was crapola with which he could do nothing.

I was beginning to feel like that hapless singer people are doing their best to avoid. There are ho-hum painters, unexciting filmmakers, and derivative writers, but the lousy musician is in a special category because a four-minute song so thoroughly assaults its listeners' environment. It can be awkward, embarrassing, and almost painful for the listener. As George Bernard Shaw once observed: "Hell is full of musical amateurs."

After an intense week of hammering away at new songs every morning, I was feeling spent by the process. "Honey from the Sky," an overcast dirge despite its title, was mostly done, but it was so gloomy that I didn't have the fortitude to play it any more. "Winner Take All," a brand new, cheerful pop item, also seemed complete, but whether or not it was any good I had no idea. I liked the idea behind the title, which fuses the "first past the post" electoral system (not always so democratic) with the image of successful individuals who succeed at everything (not always so fairly).

I emailed "Winner" to Jo, and she never got back to me. Was that a thumbs-down? One never knew with Jo until you forced the issue in person.

I finally did. We met at the Claremont, in that border-land on Sherbrooke Street between the tony Westmount neighbourhood and rough-at-the-edges NDG. Half a block east and you're in Westmount, dominated by luxury SUVS and Louis Vuitton handbags. To the west is NDG, including the Claremont, which is sandwiched between a Korean restaurant and a pharmacy, with a dance studio overhead and a gritty bar, appropriately called Liquid Lounge, nearby. With its large red sign and a black-and-white-striped awning, the Claremont occupies a neutral zone between Westmount and NDG. Inside the restaurant, one can find both designer handbags and tattoos. Jo, for example, had both.

She showed up with her usual electrifying smile and sassy demeanour. For the occasion, I'd photocopied an ad from *American Songwriter*, a magazine I'd recently purchased for the first time, to get into the spirit of things.

Clearly there is a large constituency of wannabe

songwriters out there, at least in Nashville. The magazine runs profiles of artists new and old—the usual material, except for the odd trick of the trade I didn't already know about. One ad caught my eye: "The Song Doctor—Dr. Zack Van Arsdale." The photo showed a genial-looking grey-haired man in a lab coat, a stethoscope around his neck and an acoustic guitar in his hand.

"The Cure for What Ails Your Song," trumpeted the ad. The good doc offered "Lyric and Melody Therapy," among other curative techniques. Somewhat puzzling was "Plugging Services."

"Wow, he's got a stethoscope and everything," said Jo.

"Maybe I should get a consultation."

"You should! He's in Nashville."

"I can see it now, Dr. Zack taking the blood pressure of one of my songs. 'Well, you've got 182 BPMs here. That's on the high side of normal. You're going to have to cut down on your reverb or else go on pitch-correction meds.'"

Jo wondered whether the Song Doctor would employ a defibrillator for one of my catatonic tunes.

"One verse of 'Honey from the Sky' and he'd be giving me mouth-to-mouth," I said.

After lunch we walked over to a nearby shop that sells sound systems. Jo was in the market for stereo speakers. As she shopped, I browsed docking stations for the iPhone and test-drove an impressive zeppelin-shaped model.

I played a medley of songs from my smartphone—Daniel Lanois, Massive Attack, Mick Harvey, Al Green—and then, what the hell, I cued up Krantzberg's rough mix of "Another Man's Crime." Just guitar, voice, and drums—but it sounded credible.

The music-loving salesman wore a question mark on his face. He asked, "Who's this?"

Jo smiled. She pointed to me.

ONLY ONE ARTICLE in *American Songwriter* was of interest to me. It was an interview with Donald Fagen of the jazz-laced rock band Steely Dan, which captivated audiophiles in the late 1970s and won a Grammy in 2001 for Album of the Year.

Q: Does songwriting get easier?

A: No, it gets harder. It takes longer. When you get older, your mind slows down and you don't have a lot of energy, and you've used up a lot of your ideas. You've really got to work to do it. It's exhausting. You think sitting in a room and thinking things would be easy, but it's not. I throw out so much stuff, that to get a few bars or a few good lines takes a long time.

Fagen looked very tired and not terribly happy in the accompanying photo.

My song surgeon, Jo, finally emailed me her prognosis of my latest melodic afflictions, "Honey from the Sky" and the poppy "Winner Take All."

"This is really good," she said of "Honey from the Sky." Her only suggestion was to throw in an extra chord after the chorus. As for "Winner Take All," it apparently had "potential," but the verse progression got tiresome. She suggested I replace an A with an F-sharp. Tried it. No solution. She articulated all that was troubling me about the song. The verse was hopelessly hackneyed. I texted her my thanks but mentioned that her recommended fixes did not help matters.

"That's what you get when your musical medical degree is from the Caribbean," she replied. "Maybe u should get a second opinion from the arse." (As in Van Arsdale, the Nashville Song Doctor.)

"I'm going to throw out 'Winner Take All' (that fucking loser of a song)," I wrote back, "and let 'Honey from the Sky' marinate."

"'Honey' is def a keeper," she texted.

But I felt spent by the process. I'd wasted countless hours over the past week playing "Winner Take All," trying to improve it, getting it to a point that seemed to work, a point that actually provided me with some visceral pleasure — or not quite pleasure, maybe, but getting something off my chest. But I'd rather have decompressed in front of the TV than beavered away at a song that never was going to be a song.

UNSTOPPABLE

I NEARLY WENT TO open mic night at Shäika Café, but just changing the strings on my guitar tuckered me out. Jo bailed too. She herself had no desire to perform, it seemed. Though she did manage to ask me:

"Do you ever let your fantasies run wild about all this?"

"About all what?"

"Music."

"Well, fantasize in what way?"

"Like playing Wembley Stadium or somewhere."

"No."

"You're so damn realistic."

Realistically, it felt like a breakthrough week. Jo agreed to sing "Basement Rainbow," and I booked more time at Studio Krantzberg. I tried to get her to sing another song, but she seemed to think "Rainbow" was the only tune she could manage. Regardless, I wanted to introduce her to

Krantzberg so she could make a demo with him and get somewhere worthy of her talent.

She emailed me a whaddya-think song with an alluring melody that she sang with temporary, makeshift lyrics. I told her that it worked from A to Z, had good forward motion, and only awaited the lyrics.

"Really???? I'm so glad!" she replied. "Went a little out on a limb here . . . yes, lyrics, dammit."

I told her that I'd be happy to take a stab at lyrics if she were to give me a theme. I'd extended this offer before, and she hadn't taken me up on it. But this time, for some reason, she gave the green light.

Her theme: "Well, should be right up your alley actually, all about sacrificing the search for love for art, or some other mission. Sublimation, letting go of romantic fairy tales and striving for more. Ambition, maybe? Self-actualization? It should be tough, but not cold. Should sound resolute but not cynical."

I had my marching orders. The title she'd initially used was "Unstoppable," and I was taking most of my cues from that word. I listened to her smartphone recording again and again, trying to fit words into the mosaic of her phrasing. And I pestered her with musical questions about the resolution of the chorus.

"Just gimme lyrics," she texted. "Please."

So I came up with the following pretty quickly:

UNSTOPPABLE (LYRICS FOR JO'S SONG)

You're always calling when you come up for air
after sucking it right out of me

I know you're on a mission to get everyone to listen
but I'm no longer able to feel

All that I can hear is the sound of wings beating over-
*   head, in the dark*
all that you are riding is a star that is drifting away,
*   from my heart*

Everybody gives you the time
ripped from your own headlines
you can only be seen when you are moving

And I know that gravity won't stop you
someone else will be there when you fall
I hope that you keep going till you become once and for all
unstoppable

It was a determined effort to write lyrics that would go with her sensibilities. And it was liberating to write for someone else's earworm. Not to have to be responsible for the thing. Not to have to pour my heart and soul into the alphabet and fret over the musical implications. It was work all the same, but if she liked the lyrics I could simply leave them to her own devices.

The text verdict rolled in: "Nice! Will have to play around with them to cram into my phrasing, but lots of stuff there that I like!"

Did she really mean it? I had no idea. She did employ two exclamation marks. But maybe she was being polite.

In any case, I had other irons in the fire. My meeting with Bilerman was set for 1:30 p.m.

WHO IS HOWARD BILERMAN?

I DROVE TO THE hipster district of Mile End to meet Howard
Bilerman at his studio, Hotel2Tango. A recording studio
does not generally publicize its address. It contains a ton of
expensive gear that would make thieves and musicians alike
foam at the mouth. Hotel2Tango is located in a dilapidated
part of town, on the very edge of Mile End, along a stretch
of weathered red brick industrial buildings that have gone
through a cycle of boom, bust, and bohemianism.

There was parking in the rear of the building, beside a
trailer daubed with psychedelic graffiti and caked with old
snow. More graffiti on a rust-coloured brick wall. And all the
cars in the lot, mine included, had that Soviet-grey patina
that the worst of winter brings out.

I buzzed the "hotel" button on the intercom, and a man
I took to be Bilerman answered. He was in his early forties,
with black horn-rimmed glasses, dark thinning hair, and a
lavender shirt collar poking out of his sweater. He cut the

über-relaxed figure of someone who might be the software programmer of a Brooklyn start-up.

"Let me give you a quick tour," he said. After Krantzberg's cramped basement, this felt like a visit to Hearst Castle. Bilerman led me through a room with a kitchenette, espresso machine, small dining table, desktop computer, and pinball machine. He opened a heavy door with a sign that read, CHILDREN ARE ALLOWED BUT MUST BE SEATED. We entered the cavernous recording room, its walls lined with guitar amps, effects pedals, and a motley collection of keyboard instruments. In one alcove, shiny drums, cymbals, and mic stands were strewn about; nearby was a cluster of guitars on stands; and in another area stood an organ bought from a church before it was converted to condos.

Decor was provided by a pink Victorian couch, a couple of faded oriental rugs, and various retro signs and posters, including a huge one depicting a scantily clad circus lady and a tiger. The Rolling Stones circa 1971 would have been very comfortable here. So was I.

Bilerman's tour ended in the control room. No laptop taking care of business there. A gigantic mixing board with miles of faders and a vast acreage of knobs and buttons stretched out before me; there were stacks of rack-mounted outboard gear, reel-to-reel tape machines, and tape—actual magnetic tape. I admired the sonic wonderland.

Bilerman sat down on a swivel chair, and checked the time on his phone. "I can give you thirty minutes," he said. Were anyone else to say as much, it would have sounded like my-time-is-money condescension. But coming from him it seemed courteous and efficient.

I took a seat on a black leather couch, my shoes on an

oriental throw rug, and began my pitch. I dislike having to pitch and was feeling apprehensive about it, already exhausted by the process of pitching, which I had not had to do for some time: to hustle your talents, such as they are, to feel the clock advancing while you stumble on some issue or get bogged down in idle chit-chat that takes you off course, to be judged partially on your merits but more on what the other party has already decided before you even walked into the room, based on some boss-man's flavour of the month or proverbial "candidate in mind," and going through the motions of a fair hearing that is in fact a charade. Or the exercise might be authentic, and you have to sweat out your pitch, hit all the right notes in the right key.

I didn't miss that sort of thing. But at least here I was talking about music. No longer was I selling my soul for some glossy magazine story or vacuous docudrama. This was music. And even if I was an outsider, I had twelve notes in my heart and felt privileged to be talking about the stuff.

I reiterated what I'd emailed Bilerman: that I had a batch of songs and wanted to record one or two of them with him, or a dozen, if that turned out to be possible. I let him know that I wasn't much of a singer, but that I hoped to press some good singers I knew into service. I'd been planning to record my songs for many months, I told Bilerman, and when I'd mentioned the idea to musicians, his name had come up more than once.

The name hadn't meant anything to me at first.

"Let me guess," one musician friend had said, "you're working with Howard Bilerman?"

"No," I replied, "I never heard of Howard Bilerman."

When another acquaintance from an entirely different walk of life heard about my songs and my efforts to get them properly recorded, he also wondered if I'd considered working with Howard Bilerman.

"Who is Howard Bilerman?" I asked.

I got a sketchy answer: A drummer. A producer. Something about Arcade Fire.

I learned that once upon a time he'd indeed played drums with homegrown sensation Arcade Fire, did most of their engineering, and co-mixed their breakout record, *Funeral*. Now he was producing and engineering a ton of artists; his website plastered dozens of album covers like so many hockey cards. I gave some of those artists a listen on iTunes, liked a lot of what I'd heard, was impressed with the wide range of genres—from country to klezmer to pop—and purchased a raft of songs by excellent artists I'd never heard of, like The Wooden Sky, Basia Bulat, Cœur de Pirate, and Vic Chesnutt. I'd been playing a CD that I'd burned and titled "Bilerman Mix."

When I finished my spiel, he told me that he first got into recording music as a teenager by taping concerts with a microphone, mixer, and tape deck at clubs like Foufounes Électriques so he could see shows for free. His production approach, then as now, was to make recordings as "live" as possible. At Hotel2Tango he used various technologies, magnetic tape as well as hard-drive computer recording, but the technology wasn't his main concern. His thing was "capturing live performance" and trying to get it as real and natural as possible. To hear Bilerman tell it, he isn't much more than a sonic looking glass. But he's made about four hundred records. And passive mirrors don't manage to pull that off. He obviously brings smarts and taste to the mixing console.

"I'm glad to hear that you're not fixated on one particular album that I've made," he said. "Because people often come in here thinking that I have some gold dust I can just sprinkle on them, make their record sell. But your record is going to be a reflection of you and your songs. I have no gold dust."

In his view, the best recordings are those in which the artists have everything worked out in advance, and the magic of a good performance can be captured in studio. He didn't rule out adding material in the studio after the initial recording, but the emphasis on live performance was key. "It's just that the audience won't get to hear the performance until months after it takes place."

"The trouble is," I said, "I'm not in a band. I can't create that kind of performance magic in the studio. I'm going to have to find and drag other musicians in one by one."

"Every record is different," he acknowledged.

Meanwhile, the pitch clock was ticking. I asked if he wanted to hear some of my songs and booted up my laptop. I started with "Basement Rainbow," just voice and guitar — a live performance, as it turned out, captured in the Krantzberg Ballroom. Bilerman listened patiently. Before the song came to an end, I opened another file and played "Another Man's Crime."

I mentioned that I saw this one song as a soulful tune, that I was hoping to get an R&B singer for it, and that I had bold plans for a horn section to punch the chorus in particular, and that a bass with groove was obviously desperately needed.

But he waved all that away, telling me that I clearly had a handle on songcraft, that my songs were good, and that I knew what I was doing. I only half heard his kind words. I can't recall exactly what he was saying, but it was flattering.

"It reminds me of Townes Van Zandt, though you don't actually sound like him," he said.

I was ashamed to say that I knew the name but not the music. "There are all sorts of gaping holes in my pop culture consciousness."

Bilerman said that if a song worked, it worked on its own, just like my stripped-down versions. You can always layer and add and embellish. But songs that work, work in their most basic form. My songs worked, he said, as "Country Mile" played on my laptop and I wished it was Jo singing it.

He told a story of how his young daughter had recently made a drawing and he photographed it at every stage of creation. The girl kept adding designs. He was able to go back later and look at every stage of the additions. "At a certain point I could point to the drawing and say: she should have stopped here! That's the challenge always, figuring out when to stop." It was like cooking. You have to know when to stop adding ingredients.

Bilerman seemed interested in working together. Maybe he seemed that way to everyone.

"One, two songs?" I asked. "How might we proceed?"

"You might as well do more than that, as just setting up takes a fair bit of time," he said.

I asked about other musicians, that I was in need of some. He described himself as a good resource for finding musicians. And when I praised some of the bands he'd produced, The Wooden Sky among them, Bilerman said that they would make a good backing band for me. They were in Toronto but came to town a lot.

He suggested I send him my songs. He'd give them a listen when he did his long drives to upstate New York to pick up magnetic tape.

Bilerman had to get going to pick up the little crayon artist who kept adding and adding to her masterpieces. We walked over to our respective winter-grey vehicles and said goodbye. The sky was cloudless and it was mighty cold, what felt like the coldest day of the year. Things would move faster with Bilerman. And differently, somehow. I wanted to book a room at Hotel2Tango, with its weathered sofa, faded rugs, and laid-back analogue grandeur. I wanted to be thrown into the crucible of performance.

I headed down Rue St-Urbain, eyeing the whimsical minaret and dome of the Byzantine-style church on St-Viateur, the street where I used to live alongside Hasidim and Hellenics and hipsters. I passed Tommy the barber, who could always be counted on for wacky chatter and a wonky haircut. I still had a soft spot for Tommy, though for some time I had avoided walking by his shop, embarrassed that I switched allegiances to a more upscale salon. I turned down Avenue du Parc and swivelled to look at a man at the No. 80 bus stop who was dressed in a leopard-print parka and playing what seemed to be a miniature black saxophone. The sight was so outlandish that I nearly slammed into the car stopped at a light in front of me.

In my incandescent state of mind following Hotel2Tango, I interpreted the oddly dressed sax player as a sign that I should be recording with Bilerman, in this part of town.

I decided to make an excursion over to the city's best-stocked magazine shop, the Multimags on Avenue du Mont-Royal. The air was brutal as I crossed the street, cold that bites a layer off your face, but I stopped to gaze at a weird window display in a second-hand CD shop adjacent to Multimags. It contained dozens of little replica guitars of all makes, all perfectly true to the real thing: Fender Telecasters, Gibson SGs, and so on, each with a tag identifying the famous Santana or Clapton associated with the actual guitar. Above the garden of bonsai guitars was a selection of showcased CDs. My eye caught the the cover of a Cœur de Pirate album, a frothy pop record I had just mentioned to Bilerman as one of his productions that I liked.

Another sign that my musical fate, such as it was, lay with Bilerman? I seemed to be in the mood for signs. In the magazine shop I grabbed a newspaper and then meandered over to the music section. One magazine lured me: *Songlines,* a world beat publication that I wasn't familiar with, a high-production affair that came with a CD. I'm not sure why I decided to buy it in such a sight-unseen manner, but I did, and flipped through a few of the pages in a card-shuffling way. A small photo of a bespectacled man caught my eye.

Bilerman?

It couldn't be. I searched back for the page, found it, saw the little photo again, and voilà: the cutline referred to one Howard Bilerman. The picture accompanied a feature story about the Malian artist Kouyaté, whose record he had produced. Another sign.

BASEMENT SESSION NO. 4

A GUITAR PICK DOES not break easily. In fact it's only happened to me twice in my life, the first time on the
day I began recording with Krantzberg. Hurriedly getting
my gear together, I grabbed a black pick and unthinkingly
squeezed it between my thumb and index finger, perhaps
out of pre-recording stage fright, or possibly to gauge its
firmness (there are many gradations). It snapped in two. This
seemed like a freak accident and, if I were being pessimistic,
a bad sign. I reserved judgement. That first Krantzberg session turned out to be good and bad. Overall it got the ball
rolling and showed me what I needed to do better. I kept
the broken pick as a talisman.

And now it happened again, in much the same fashion,
on the way to my first Krantzberg session after his return
from Anaheim. My pick of choice — a grey Jim Dunlop
nylon plectrum, .88 millimetres thick, which is a medium-
hard firmness — snapped in my fingers.

And as with that first studio session, a snowstorm was once again underway. It was a high-calibre February snow, soft beneath sunny skies no longer packing a windy punch. It was different from the mean-spirited weather of the past month. And as with that first session, I would be missing the snow show, once again holed up in Eli Krantzberg's basement.

This time with Jo. She had agreed to sing one of my songs, just one, though I'd believe it when I saw it, as she so often opted out of plans on account of being a single mom and a real estate agent on call. Plus she had mixed feelings about singing with me. "I want to do my own stuff," she'd tell me whenever I suggested we jam. There was more and more of her stuff. She was on a songwriting roll.

But I persisted in asking her to sing one of my songs in the studio. I promised to make her famous—"or vice versa." She finally took the bait, probably more curious to see how she would feel in a studio than eager to actually sing one of my songs.

"Bring your golden pipes," I texted on my way to pick her up.

She seemed in good spirits as we motored through NDG, resplendent in its fresh garb of snow. Krantzberg welcomed us and remarked on my nylon guitar case.

"Nice guitar bag," he said.

"Thanks. It's run of the mill. But it has straps so that it works as a backpack."

"I haven't seen one like that in ages."

"I have a soft spot for knapsacks and bags with lots of zippers and compartments," I said. "I can walk by scores of clothing shops and not really notice anything. But show me a knapsack or a computer bag with nifty pockets…"

Krantzberg told me he felt the same way, and got out a bag he'd recently acquired. I liked its features and remarked on how good it would be for air travel.

"You guys," said Jo, feigning a yawn. "This is really rock 'n' roll."

"It's hardly fair," I said, "that women get to walk around with contraptions that hold things, while men are expected to stuff everything into their pockets."

Krantzberg agreed. "Especially with cellphones now. Who wants to walk around with one of these things" — he waved his new smartphone — "in their pocket?"

"It's cumbersome," I said.

"It doesn't look good," he said.

Jo appeared ready to leave.

"Can I get you something to drink?" Krantzberg asked her. "Some tea?"

We descended to the basement, Krantzberg following several minutes later with a cup of Earl Grey for the guest singer. Jo seemed pleased in the studio environment and marvelled over his gleaming drum kit.

"So what song are we going to do?" Krantzberg asked.

The answer was "Basement Rainbow," which at this stage consisted of just my acoustic guitar and vocals, plus a click track. This had always been Jo's favourite of my tunes; her voice would replace mine.

Krantzberg set up the mic and pop shield (a circular piece of nylon mounted over the microphone to eliminate popping sounds) and a music stand to hold lyrics; he handed out headphones and took up his usual position, his back to me, as he faced the computer.

He got Jo to sing a bit so he could adjust the levels. Then he played back my rhythm guitar track. Jo threw her voice into the equation. I wondered whether she would go off on acrobatic phrasing tangents, perhaps to spite what she has often described as my "male" approach to singing, perhaps to put her own stamp on things. But she proved fairly faithful to my vocal version.

Thrilled as I was that she was actually singing one of my songs, I walked on eggshells when it came to making suggestions. I crossed out one word from the lyric sheet where I thought she was going too slowly through the words and missing the boat on my phrasing. A couple of times I felt she came in too late or didn't linger over a word as I would. But she did a sublime job, and splitting hairs over a few lines where she took liberties would be ungrateful and—knowing her—useless.

For example, when I sang "trembling ruins," I made the *trembling* tremble, dragging the word out in shaky way. I suggested as much to her. I even noted that J. S. Bach often coloured phrasing in this way so that the music would animate a word or idea. She demurred.

She did two takes, probably one more than absolutely necessary. But Krantzberg liked to have extra material in case problems arose later that might require digital cutting and pasting. Her exquisite vocals were now safely stored in that stylish bag, replete with zippers, pockets, and hidden pouches, that is a digital audio workstation. It was in the can.

I found myself way ahead of schedule. Dare I try to get her to do another song? I dared, and she agreed to sing "Country Mile," though she was skeptical. This recording was even more enjoyable: she was singing not just to my acoustic guitar, but also to Krantzberg's terrific drumming as well as his piano playing, which texturized the chorus. And I'd always loved the sweet, delicate, quasi-country way she sang this song.

I think she resisted partly because of the lyrics. "Country Mile" is about Nathalie; it's the song for which finding a chorus had given me so much grief—the song that launched a dozen tunes.

When Jo went over the lyrics, she took issue with the last verse, which begins, *I gave it lots of thought / but it tore me apart / I miss you and I always will.*

"This is not a line a woman would ever sing," Jo said.

"Why not?"

"Giving it lots of thought? You don't do that with love."

But I had done it. "How do you think," I said, "I got to be my age without ever having been married?"

She laughed and proceeded to lay down her vocal track. I was so pumped to hear it that I was bopping around and bumped my head on one of the ceiling's low-lying exposed pipes. Captain K. hit the stop button on the Starship Enterprise. His ears miss nothing. Another run-through while I tried not to throw a wrench into the works. I had found a plastic back-scratcher and was using it as a maestro's baton to signal entry points and solo breaks. But Jo vetoed the back-scratcher, saying it was too comical. I mostly kept out of harm's way until the final chorus, where the line *easier for you to walk away* is repeated four times, unbeknownst to Jo. I gesticulated wildly to indicate repetition and whispered the word *again*; she got it, and delivered a stellar coda to the song.

Krantzberg, however, removed his headphones and reported that my *again* had been captured by the microphone. "We'll have to do it again, or at least the ending," he said.

But Jo had executed it so beautifully, so organically. Even she agreed. "Can't you just excise my *again*?" I asked.

Dr. Krantzberg, unfazed, went back into the lab, pouring admixtures in and out of digital test tubes. Yes, he concluded, my utterance was positioned in such a way that it could be airbrushed from history, though some intake of the singer's breath would also disappear in the process.

Two lead vocals were as much as I could expect from Jo, so I asked whether she might try some backups. She was game. We cued up "Another Man's Crime." I had the idea to generate some *ooohs* over the pre-chorus section. When I attempted an example she looked at me as if my idea was not so much Tin Pan Alley as tin ear. But I urged her to try anyway, which she did, applying a very thin coat of *ooohs* over the drywall chords.

What followed was a thickly painted wall of sound, and Krantzberg rose to the occasion, showing himself to be a first-rate choirmaster when it came to building lush backups. After Jo laid down her tentative backing vocal *ooohs*, Krantzberg swivelled his chair around and briskly asked her to double it. Jo obliged. He then suggested she try to harmonize on it, and then that was followed by another doubling. Tripling ensued. And then the choirmaster suggested she go up an octave, icing on a multi-layered cake.

Over the last verse I had Jo cooing "Another Man's Crime," and it went fast and left me feeling rapturous. It all sounded pretty sweet in playback, as if my creaky, arthritic vocals were getting massaged by a vast number of very sultry, soft, feminine fingers.

HOOKS

I SLEPT WELL THAT night, enjoying the peace of mind that comes with song progress. But the weather was out of sync with my mood. A rain-hail-snow concoction had plummeted to the ground. Every street corner was a profound mud puddle with the consistency of hummus. Trail-blazers searched for alternate routes across the street. Young people jumped. Old folks were stranded on street corners waiting for good Samaritans. Laundry hampers filled with mud-splotched jeans, and dry cleaners did brisk business.

I wondered about the songs. There was a timing problem with the guitar in one spot where Jo sang over "Basement Rainbow"—not enough breathing space between lines— and it spoiled the recording for me.

I emailed Morey up there in his tower of song, sending him the two tracks Jo had sung. He liked "Country Mile," said it sounded great and was keen to hear it with more instruments. "Basement Rainbow," however, left him cold. I appreciated his honesty and told him I welcomed any suggestions.

"I'm not sure why this song doesn't grab me as much as the other one," he replied. "I think it's just that the 'flow' isn't as smooth for me. It's like it's missing some fluidity and is unfinished in a way—the hook isn't apparent—but I'm anxious to see what you'll do to flesh it out."

His use of the word *hook* stood out. I'd always thought a hook was a catchy instrumental riff that sometimes kicked off a song and showed up after the chorus. Yet recently I'd read references to hooks in the verse, in the pre-chorus, in the chorus, after the chorus—more hooks than a pirate ship. What was with all the hookification? What did Morey mean by a hook not being apparent? I emailed him back my question.

"By 'hook' I mean that there isn't as strong a transition from verse to chorus which 'lifts.' Something that is 'catchy' and sticks in the brain—something to sing along to…"

That added new criteria to my idea of good songwriting. The entire song, it seemed, would have to "hook" the listener in.

Or as Morey put at the end of his email: "You get five minutes or less to build a strong foundation of some sonic architecture, a layered canvas of music that needs to make someone 'feel' something—it's a challenge but so satisfying when you think you've got something there."

What was that something? I told myself it's whatever makes the song work—the way anything else in life works properly, gets from A to B, becomes a decent example of whatever it aspires to. But with music, successfully getting from A to B is often a matter of personal taste.

Meanwhile, Morey's music had lately been reflecting a change in personal taste. His daughter, Hayley, was precociously gaga over Radiohead, the brilliant, world-weary English rock band. During the past couple of months, father and daughter had recorded and uploaded to YouTube a half-dozen Radiohead songs. These covers showed a more confident Hayley singing to very intricate instrumental tracks that Morey was mapping out with great narrative skill. The Richmans had come a long way in just a few months since their first, badly-lit video featured a shy Hayley singing Christina Aguilera's "Beautiful" against the basic backdrop of Morey's acoustic guitar.

As for my own songs, missing hooks and all, some welcome news landed:

"These are really great."

Bilerman says he likes my songs.

That was the news flash that made my week. Maybe my year. After our meeting a week earlier, Bilerman had suggested I send him some songs. So I sent him half a dozen, including the two I'd gotten Jo to sing in Krantzberg's studio.

This was his reply by email:

these are really great...

i'm torn in terms of voice. I really like the way you sing your songs...like I said last week...honest & free of artifice.

having said that, the woman singing on those 2 does have a very lovely voice.

one way or another, she should definitely be singing
in there somewhere. maybe harmonies?

Bilerman and Morey seemed to occupy opposite ends of
the recording spectrum. Bilerman advocated performance
in a living, breathing, "honest and free of artifice" fashion.
Morey, though he can play guitar in real time with the best
of them, employed all manner of sampled sounds in his laptop studio. (I never asked him, but I was quite sure Morey
would not have recommended that I record my own voice,
free of artifice though it might have been. I suspected he'd
advise some artifice.)

Where did I stand? I wasn't in a band, and therefore
was not in a position to hone my tunes with other musicians and have Bilerman simply press the Record button
in Hotel2Tango and bottle the magic. So that forced me to
do "overdubs" (layer instruments one at a time in a multi-
track recording). Bilerman was not dogmatic; he agreed.
But he still wanted to capture what's known as the "bed
tracks"—drums, bass, guitar, and maybe vocals—in live-
performance fashion.

I bumped into a neighbour on the street, and a talk about
how the Montreal Canadiens were faring morphed into a
talk about music. He cycled through a few topics and then
slammed U2. "Without all their fancy little tricks in the studio and ten different producers, they'd be nothing," he said.

I'd never owned a U2 album, except for one that I
received when I was working as a music critic, but I found
his assessment harsh. If a song works, you can strip away all
its bells and whistles, undress the thing, and there it will lie
before you, naked as the day it entered the world, a natural

beauty. On that score, I thought both Morey and Bilerman would agree.

But what about the "fancy little tricks," the layers, the clothing? Did I want my songs to walk around as they would on a tropical beach? Just me and my guitar and my subpar but (as Bilerman put it) *honest* voice, along with bass and drums, all hugging the coastline of the tune in a real live performance? Or should the songs be wrapped in innumerable layers, as Montrealers must dress this time of year? Michelin Man versus Beach Dude. My singing seemed nowhere near good enough to strut those songs around in the buff.

Bilerman sent me a copy of an email he'd sent to his studio partner, Thierry, a bass player. Bilerman described my songs as "beautiful" and wondered whether his partner was interested in playing bass on the tunes. I did not ask whether Bilerman himself was thinking of handling the drums.

His bassist colleague played in bands with infinitely more alternative, envelope-pushing material than my songs could offer. Just the names of his bands made the point quite eloquently: Godspeed You! Black Emperor and Thee Silver Mt. Zion Memorial Orchestra. The latter combo is described as "post-rock." I wasn't sure how well his sensibilities would mesh with homespun tunes that were less than trail-blazing.

I had to leave that dilemma for the time being; Jo and I had a lunch planned, if she didn't cancel. And I had a bone to pick with her.

She had recently emailed me the latest version of her new song, "Unstoppable," mentioning that although she really liked my lyrics, she did not use them. Her song may have been hit material, but I'd worked hard on those lyrics;

they were made for measure, made for her, and it royally disappointed me that she haughtily cast them aside. When I emailed to ask why, she put it down to phrasing. She was going to keep them for another occasion, so she said. Last time I'd write words for her.

BASEMENT BASS 'N' DRUMS

HOW WAS IT THAT every time I had a session scheduled at Studio Krantzberg there was a snowstorm? I wasn't complaining. The late-February snowfall, warming things up as with all snowfalls, was pulling the city out of the doldrums of extreme cold, nasty winds, and bleak skies. The snow settled with stick-to-it-iveness, prettily lining tree branches and wrought-iron railings.

"It's always interesting to finally see what people look like after you've imagined them," said Peter Wilson.

We were in Krantzberg's subterranean studio. Wilson had played bass alongside Krantzberg in their wedding band for decades and had been recommended as someone who might lay down some basslines for my songs.

When it came to imagining the composer, Wilson had only two songs to go on. He'd figured I was about thirty years old and had some sort of "half beard" on my face. He didn't mention a tattoo. But I got his drift. He'd expected me to look hipper.

I took this more as a compliment to my songs than an insult to my person. And I made a mental note not to shave on the mornings of future recording sessions.

Wilson himself was fiftyish, tall, with angular features and a string-bean build. He was wearing a plaid shirt, dark cargo pants, and grey sandals with socks. His most fashionable accessories were his rectangular glasses and his instrument, a caramel-coloured bass boasting five strings and a cutaway body shape.

This marked the first time I'd ever paid a musician to play on one of my songs. It went against my hope to assemble a volunteer brigade of friends motivated by the sheer love of music-making. But it slowly became clear that my pickings were to be slim unless I kicked in some cash incentive for bass and drums, not to mention luxury items like horns.

And Wilson's price was more than fair. I had emailed the bassist two partial recordings along with a rudimentary description of the chord changes. Now he set up two sheets of paper on a music stand, his "sketches" of my songs. This was elegant to behold: notes written out on music paper lined with music staves; the title—*Country Mile, E. Siblin*; and a time signature and other musically literate markings that were so much advanced algebra to me.

Krantzberg got his sonic spaceship up and running with his usual efficiency. Wilson occupied a stool, put on headphones, and warmed up briefly to "Country Mile." I was impressed with what I heard. We discussed a few issues, such as when the bass should come in. Then our engineer hit the Record button and Wilson laid down his bassline.

I was enjoying it too much to pay strict attention. I liked what he'd come up with and felt a visceral delight at hearing a song of mine sung by Jo, with Krantzberg doing superb drum duty, plus acoustic guitar, piano, and now a bass anchoring the thing, turning it into a bona fide song.

By the second take it was a *fait accompli*. The next song, "Another Man's Crime," required more discussion. There is an extended section for a solo break, followed by a verse where I wanted the song to break open before gathering steam for a big chorus and fade-out.

Wilson mapped out his excellent bassline. I noticed Krantzberg's toe tapping out a rhythm. The soulful scaffolding I'd hoped for was in place. Two takes and we gave it a listen. Despite having entered the trancelike state that comes over me whenever I'm thoroughly enjoying music, I forced myself to concentrate and was able to hear one tiny spot where the bass faltered. I pointed it out, and we agreed to have Wilson "punch in" a correction on that spot. He had to dive into the song partway through and play that problem part right, with his entry point right on the mark and his exit similarly flawless. It took several attempts.

"It's nerve-wracking," Wilson said afterwards. I was surprised: he'd appeared so masterfully calm.

He packed up his caramel-coloured five-string bass. Because he had graciously offered me his first hour in the studio for free, my tab for his laying down basslines for two songs in about forty-five minutes was precisely zero. I paid him something more reasonable.

"It was fun working on your songs," he said.

Upstairs, Krantzberg's fiancée was chatting with a girl-friend, and we joined them, partaking in Mariam's lemon cake. Her studio is the kitchen. "Let's just say Eli doesn't go hungry," she told me. Now I learned about the theme parties she regularly threw. Wilson had been to her "pink" party, where guests had to dress accordingly. There had also been a *Mad Men* party, among others. I could see Krantzberg and Mariam enjoyed life.

I was curious about how Krantzberg had come to music, drums, and digital recording. I knew he didn't have musical roots in his family, because he'd emailed me an article he'd written about his late father. Morris Krantzberg had immigrated to Canada from Russia at the age of four. He served in the Royal Canadian Air Force during the Second World War, specializing in radar. After a stint running a small-town grocery store, the elder Krantzberg opened what became a popular children's shoe store on Queen Mary Road, Kiddie Kobbler. (As a kid I'd been fitted for shoes there on numerous occasions.) From a young age, Eli Krantzberg was expected to go into the family biz.

"So how was it you started playing drums?" I asked him once as I sat in his living room, sipping a cup of rooibos tea he'd made. His reply took me by surprise.

"My parents came up with the idea of drums as a sort of therapy," he said, "a constructive way to get the aggression out of me."

This did not square with my impression of the soft-spoken, patient, courteous man I'd come to know. But Krantzberg explained that at the age of nine he was angered when his grandmother died and he only found out about it after he got home from summer camp.

"It was a dramatic death," he said. "She died in a car accident, and I'd been really close to her. Looking back, I was having trouble emotionally. Drums was a good thing to have me focus on...I took a few lessons but gave it up, the way kids of ten do."

A few years later, hanging out with friends in the high school band room, he fooled around on a drum kit. A teacher heard him, was impressed, and suggested he take a music course as an elective.

In high school he continued to work part-time in the family shoe store, but by Grade 9 he was hooked on drums and getting good, under the influence of progressive rock bands like Genesis and Yes. He soon formed a band of his own. The guitarist, a classmate, was one Morey Richman.

The band, called Labyrinth, practiced every Friday night in the Krantzberg family basement and played parties and one memorable school concert. Krantzberg was reportedly focused and disciplined. Morey remembers the rest of the band drinking beer and partying with girls while the drummer was holed up in an upstairs room transcribing horn solos from a Chicago album.

After high school, he studied music at Vanier College, fell under the spell of jazz greats, and learned how to play the vibraphone. "I was learning all about jazz theory and getting drawn into Coltrane and Milt Jackson," he told me. "Back then, when you got into a [university] jazz program it was a very closed mentality and you focused only on jazz; you developed this 'jazz police' mentality that everything else is crap. It's also the hubris of youth, a bit."

Upon graduation, one of his teachers hired him as a drummer for a band that played downtown hotel lounges. They had long-term gigs, the first being at a top-floor circular restaurant, the Tour de Ville in the Hyatt Regency. The band played six nights a week. The repertoire was "generic hotel music" like Lionel Richie, classic waltzes, "Copacabana," and a couple of disco tunes. Then he started doing wedding gigs and discovered that he could make as much at a wedding as he could in five or six nights at hotels. Thus was born Nightshift, his seven-piece band fronted by a female singer.

"What about recording? How did you get into that?"

Krantzberg explained that while working nights as a drummer he went back to school, completing a degree in political science at Concordia University (at about the same time I was studying history there). A few years later, he did a graduate degree in communications at Concordia. Soon thereafter he discovered — and was an early adopter of — the digital audio workstation called Logic.

He remains the drummer in Nightshift, which at last count has produced a quarter-century of waltzes, horas, and golden oldies. And he channels his sound recording expertise into making instructional videos for a company called Groove3.

We'd been alone in the living room, but now I heard footsteps coming down the stairs. It was Mariam.

"Did you get to the part when his life got enormously better?" she asked. "When he met me?"

"Um, not yet," I said. "How did his life get better when he met you?"

"Better food. Better furniture."

"Keep going," I said.

"Better everything. All his basic needs taken care of," she said.

After a moment, she added, "Chili," referring to what was simmering on the stovetop. "Do you want to try some?"

A FEW DAYS after Wilson added his basslines to "Country Mile" and "Another Man's Crime," Krantzberg called to say he had a free hour and was going to lay down some final drums for those two songs. And while I may be tonally challenged, I am rhythmically oriented and opinionated. Besides, these were my songs. I wanted to be there.

We went to work on "Another Man's Crime." Krantzberg recorded a drum track that moved in lockstep with the bassline. I wasn't convinced and wondered whether he could try a more syncopated beat. I also suggested he play the chorus on the ride cymbal and throw in more fills. Krantzberg then added a smidgen of funky high-hat action here and there. In no time, he was sounding magnificent.

For the third verse I wanted the song to open up and breathe. "Would you mind," I asked him, "if I tried to play what I have in mind?" I'm no drummer, but when I was a teenager and played in some bands, parking myself behind a drum kit was a thrill I always tried to sneak in during jams and rehearsals. When the drummer took a break, I'd head straight for the stretched skins and vulcanized metal.

Krantzberg looked at me warily as I took his sticks and got behind the kit. I tentatively hit a couple of drums. It was shockingly loud. I did not remember such volume. Perhaps I'd never played such a quality kit. In any case, Krantzberg cued the section in question and I played in clumsy fashion what was dexterous in my mind.

It gave him a rough idea, and he didn't dislike it. I was producing a series of fills and landing on cymbals rather than playing a beat per se.

"Usually," he said, "it's the drummer who pushes for a drummistic part."

I gave Krantzberg back his drums. I took a seat at his controls, gazed at the rainbow of colour-coded bars on his monitor, the faders on the mixing board, the framed photo of the drummer and his sweetie on his desk.

Krantzberg activated the song with a wireless keyboard and was again laying down the drum track, incorporating all we'd hashed out. Listening to the fine results on headphones, I was starting to believe that a record might actually one day emerge.

THE GIRL FROM THE
NEXTDOOR PUB

SHAHARAH HAD HER USUAL Thursday night gig at the NextDoor Pub, so after a couple of periods of the hockey game, I ventured over to her show. I paid the ten-dollar cover, and when I walked through the door she was between sets, sitting on the stage. I screwed up some courage and introduced myself.

"I've written a song that I think would sound great with you singing it," I said.

"Oh yeah?"

"Yeah. Um, would you consider possibly singing it? I mean, you'd have to like it."

"Why don't you send me the song?" Shaharah said I could call her.

She and her band soon launched into a set, melting the paint off the walls and whipping the crowd into a dance floor frenzy. The fans looked like early adopters of a singer destined to go places. As Shaharah ruled one end of the narrow pub, the third period of the hockey game played on a screen at the other end. Many of us were torn between the funk onstage and the funk the Canadiens were getting themselves into on ice. They were blowing a 3–1 lead against the Islanders, who tied it up, throwing the game into overtime. The local team had won a startling five games in a row, so the hockey fans in the pub were emotionally invested. I swung my head back and forth between the skittering puck and the smouldering Shaharah. But the rubbernecking was getting tiresome, so I settled on a compromise. I watched the game, back turned rudely to the stage, while swaying my body to the propulsive music. It seemed to work. Except that Shaharah finished her set at the very instant that New York scored the winner in overtime.

The next day, I called her and explained where I was at in the recording process. She was very down-to-earth for a singer who has an adoring, overheated crowd in the palm of her hand every Thursday night. She suggested I email her the tune, which I later did, with foreboding. After hearing her powerful soulfulness, I feared "Another Man's Crime" would come across as amateur and plodding.

WHILE I WAS waiting for Shaharah's response, I had a question for Morey, one of many sound-design issues I'd been grappling—and pestering him—with.

Dear Morey (this is becoming a sort of Dear Abby column for a troubled songwriter...),

I'm sitting here playing electric guitar to my songs, watching the snow drift down to earth, trying to deepen the soundscapes a bit, and was wondering what effects pedal might be a good one to produce some atmospherics. Ever since I grew a beard in my early twenties, quit the band I was playing in, and put down my electric for an acoustic, I've been effects-illiterate. But I figure I should experiment and tinker some.

I realize this is a pretty vague question without you knowing precisely what atmosphere I'm going for, but any suggestions? I'd like to get away from the fact that all my songs thus far feature relentless folkified strumming.

Meanwhile, I tried some soundscaping of my own. With Krantzberg's expertise on the MIDI controller, we came up with some synthetic horns and piano for a new song, "Go Slow." It's hard to get the right horn line when you don't have a horn and you're not a horn player. But it confirmed that a trumpet suited the song.

FORTY-EIGHT HOURS AFTER I emailed Shaharah my song—no reply. In the meantime, I made surprising plans with Nathalie, she of "Country Mile." I had recently sent her an email by mistake (iBlame the iPhone) in which I mentioned lunching with Jo and having my ringer turned off. Nathalie got the wrong impression and replied a day later in a diplomatic email that mentioned she had met someone.

The upshot of the reopened communication was that we made plans to go skiing. As I drove along the Voie Camillien-Houde, the road that runs over Mont Royal, to meet her, I saw two black horses cavorting in the balmy snow, lyrical to behold even as a blur from the car window. It brought to mind the first line from "Cherries," in which (based on an old family photograph) I picture my grandfather riding horses in this very spot, with his own father.

The Led Zeppelin song "D'yer Mak'er" was playing on the radio, sending all its *oh-oh-oh-oh*s into my cerebral cortex. A song I never particularly liked, but which has always and mysteriously given me a profound case of earworm.

I found a parking spot on Avenue du Parc by the mountain. From there I could see the home where my grandfather grew up, across from what used to be called Fletcher's Field and is now Parc Jeanne-Mance, on Avenue de l'Esplanade. These days, it's home to Armand Vaillancourt, a celebrated sculptor in his eighties who in recent years has posed for fashion ads. The initials of my great-grandfather's name are welded into the cast-iron gate: HR — Harry Rosenfeld.

From my parking place, I emailed confirmation of my sessions at Hotel2Tango, nearly three months away in May. For two days I had been exchanging emails with Bilerman and his recommended bassist, Morgan Moore, and drummer, Mark "Bucky" Wheaton, trying with great difficulty to find three days when we could all play. The drummer and the bassist were each out of town for long stretches. Bilerman was booked solid for months. It was like trying to set up a meeting with a trio of busy corporate lawyers, albeit with one of them named Bucky. Finally we'd settled on a date.

The snow was heavy and wet when I met up with Nathalie on the trail above the monument. She was wearing a black ski outfit, and despite the wet conditions she glided with the smooth elegance she brought to all endeavours. When we stopped in one spot for any length of time, snow would attach to our skis like barnacles. We were soon forced to kick our skis in the air and use our poles to knock sticky clumps of snow from them. It was tough slogging but a majestic day. She told me about her new beau. I was hopeful that we could segue into a friendship of sorts. One day I would even play her "Country Mile."

THE NEXT DAY, Jo came over for coffee and music musings. She said she'd been up till 6 a.m. with a friend. I was jealous — but only because he is a guitarist and they played her songs. She gave me some feedback on that fledgling composition "Winner Take All." And she had a suggestion for "Go Slow."

Until recently, the latter song had unfortunately been titled "Cicero." Even more unfortunately, it was about Cicero, the orator killed in the last days of the late Roman Republic, in 43 BC. It was an ill-fated attempt to mourn his murder, which was carried out by a bounty hunter on the joint orders of Mark Antony and Octavian, before those two became mortal enemies.

This was not very good subject matter for a pop song. One problem was trying to find a rhyming replacement for Cicero, an issue I finally solved by rewriting the song in memory of Ian Crystal, my close friend Michael's brother, a philosophy professor who had died suddenly a couple of months earlier in New Orleans.

I barely knew Ian, but he left a strong impression on me. He'd been over to my place twice in recent years, and together with Michael we'd had long discussions around my kitchen table in which his irreverent wit was much in evidence. I was intrigued and impressed that he'd managed to pursue the life of an academic philosopher. From a modest start in suburban Chomedey, north of Montreal, he'd studied classics as an undergraduate student in Halifax, afterwards earning a Ph.D. at King's College in London. At Louisiana State University in Baton Rouge, he specialized in ancient Greek philosophy. The density of his research is conveyed by the title of the one book he published, *Self-Intellection and Its Epistemological Origins in Ancient Greek Thought*. But he was also known to let the good times roll with a drink or two, or more. He had moved into a new apartment in the Garden District of New Orleans when his landlord, entering the flat to do some painting, discovered that he'd died after the first night in his new abode. At the time of his death, Ian, who was afflicted with diabetes, was at work on a book about Plato's *Gorgias*. He was only forty-six.

I attended Ian's funeral, and his brother's eulogy provided the raw material for a new chorus to the Cicero song. "Until we meet again, dear brother," said Michael. "I will see you on the other side." With *Cicero* replacing *Go Slow*, my new chorus seemed to write itself: *Go slow if you must leave / I know we'll meet again / I will see you on the other side / be sure to leave a sign.*

Jo liked it and urged me not to mess with it too much, yet added a proviso. And therein lay the hell that awaited me. The chorus went on for too long, she opined, and ended in a hokey way. She suggested some sort of minor chord resolution, to replace what she referred to as my "Partridge Family–type" ending.

I EMAILED SHAHARAH again, assuming that she did not like my song. Her reply was a surprise:

> hey eric!
>
> sorry for the delay in getting back to you! i really like the song, great job!!...i'd definitely like to come to the studio and try it out and see what it sounds like... let me know when that would work for you :)

We made plans for her to come into the studio four days later, when I had a session booked; she felt no need to get together beforehand to jam on the tune. Shaharah seemed very tall onstage. Would she even fit into Studio Krantzberg?

WRITE YOUR OWN NO. 1 HIT!

I SPENT A GOOD chunk of the morning trying to come up with a change for "Go Slow," but it all came to naught. My issue with the song was that there was too much acoustic guitar strumming in a verse-chorus-verse-chorus Sisyphean loop. Maybe this just reflected that the song was written by one person playing guitar. When other instruments were added to the mix, hopefully I'd be able to tone down the guitar, or remove it entirely in some places.

I went so far as to consult a DVD on songwriting. Morey had recommended a website that offered instructional DVDs for guitarists. I perused the site and purchased a disc that taught songwriting for guitarists.

"*Songwriting on Guitar* reveals a truckload of guitaristic tricks of the trade that every guitar-playing songwriter should know," declared the instructor on the DVD I purchased from the site. He was from Holland and wore a button-down violet shirt. He seemed nice enough, though he was earnest, and humourless, and mispronounced key words like "groove" and "cool."

I studiously went through about a dozen instalments of the course, hoping to find what the Dutch instructor touted as "all the creative and technical insight you'll need to write your own No. 1 hit."

I'll never know how true that is, because the idea of sitting through "16 hours of video lessons, 100 pages of reference charts, and hundreds of playing examples" was daunting, even if it were to shine light on "symmetric and asymmetric shapes," "how to create strong memorable hooks," and the search for "gwoove."

As I watched the lessons, I realized, not unhappily, how instinctual songwriting is for me. To reduce it to math—tried-and-true progressions, chords that mesh with whatever keys, and "shapes" of whatever dimensions—kills the fun.

It reminded me of a Grade 1 teacher who was annoyed by my constant doodling on exercise papers and notebooks in class. I was a budding artist at the age of six, with a penchant for cartooning. Mrs. Sally, the teacher, took me aside after one class, gave me a notebook, and said that from then on I should make my drawings in this particular book and also mark down the time of day.

My first drawing was of the teacher. After class, as instructed, I showed her the notebook and my first creation. She took offence, I remember, on account of her head being smaller than the calendar on her desk. (The metal calendar base held perforated pages representing the days of the year and was in reality quite large. Mrs. Sally's head was in fact quite small.) The formalized structure took the joy out of my drawing. I never again tried my hand at visual art in any serious way. Perhaps this was the real root of my guitar playing.

Surely, though, there were tricks of the trade that could help my cause and ease the pain of half-written songs struggling for completion. So I scoured my new instructional DVD for something on modulation—changing the key of a song in midstream to ratchet up its interest. There were two sections on the subject that made perfect mathematical sense. In practice they didn't work for "Go Slow."

Meanwhile, Jo emailed me her idea to modulate the song. She sent it in a file titled "Mod Pod." And though it did not ultimately work for me, it was a far better idea than the Dutch method.

Jo was at the time starting to do some recording of her own with a cast of characters I did not know. All I knew was that one day someone would take notice. And I would take some small pleasure in having, if not discovered her, at least noted her talent and urged her to give voice to it.

TAKE ONE WITH SHAHARAH

IT WAS MEANT TO be the long-awaited, soulful rebranding of "Another Man's Crime." Shaharah was slated to go into Studio Krantzberg and try singing the song. Instead, I got this email:

> goodmorning! i pushed myself a little too hard vocally last night and am wondering if we can move our session to another day? if it's too much of an inconvenience, i can still come by and give it a try... lemme know!!

We rescheduled, but I still had time booked at Krantzberg's, so I went in with my electric guitar and some ideas. Krantzberg had just had a cavity filled and would be fine so long as his mouth remained frozen. It felt good to sling my electric guitar in a studio. I recorded a second rhythm guitar track for "Another Man's Crime," to add texture and *gwoove.* As I played I stood near Krantzberg and swayed to the rhythm.

There remained undeveloped real estate in the song where a solo break was envisioned. Having the electric guitar in my hand was too tempting. So I launched into an impromptu solo that was hit and miss. I kept playing, and Krantzberg eventually cut and pasted the best lines so that they were strung together in a coherent statement.

We then added some electric guitar to "Country Mile" where I wanted to add some thick chordal declarations on the last verse, desperate as I was to break up the monotony of my acoustic guitar. A very fly-by-the-seat-of-my-pants solo was thrown in as well. Oddly, both solos stuck. Digital editing means that you can improvise with impunity and take the best material.

THREE DAYS LATER I was back at the studio for Shaharah's session. It turned out that Krantzberg had heard her perform and met her briefly. Before she arrived, he told me he had been impressed with her singing as well as her band. He also noted her "pole-dancing" stage presence. Krantzberg is no prude, but I suppose he found her antics distracting from the music.

She arrived more like the girl next door than the girl from the NextDoor Pub, simply attired in jeans and a charcoal-grey T-shirt emblazoned with a Native headdress. Nonetheless, she exuded glamour. I gave her a sheet of lyrics.

"I hope I can sing it," she said. "I only listened to it once. And it's not in my key."

Krantzberg set up her mic, pop shield, music stand, and

headphones. He played the tune while she tested out her honeyed voice.

"Can you cue me?" Shaharah asked me. I grabbed the back-scratcher, which didn't seem to have been used since Jo and I had horsed around with it. She smiled. Krantzberg rolled the tune and I cued her entry, then did my best not to look at her so that she could focus without feeling gawked at. She sounded phenomenal, injecting the song with all the R&B soulfulness I'd heard in my head but never been able to give voice to.

There were a few tiny areas where she phrased the words differently than I had in mind. I mentioned this, though I was reticent to question her professional instincts. But she welcomed my suggestions and said she wanted to try it whatever way I had in mind. I went up to the mic and illustrated my phrasings.

Shaharah picked up my idiosyncrasies lightning-fast, incorporating them into her breathy R&B style. Supremely relaxed, occasionally texting between takes, she sang against Jo's rich harmonies, smoothing over the sharp edges of my melodies.

I sat down happily on the basement floor with the back-scratcher in my hand. I recall looking up at her and seeing a sliver of bare midriff between her jeans and T-shirt. A thumb was lodged in her front pocket.

And then it was over.

"That's it?" she asked. "You mean I'm dismissed?"

"Well, you could always stay and play tambourine or something," I said.

We saw her upstairs, Krantzberg and I, like a couple of teenagers entrusted with the responsibility of walking the school beauty queen to the general assembly stage.

And that was that. I went back downstairs to work on the song some more, and everything in the tune glowed in her wake. Krantzberg played some fat Rhodes piano chords for the chorus resolutions and slid in some organ beneath the solo break. The song now had added texture as well as top-drawer vocals. Then I tried another long-standing fantasy for "Another Man's Crime," a horn section. But the song didn't benefit from the sampled horn sounds. Evidently not all the theoretical sounds in my head translated well in practice.

A DAY LATER, I found myself feeling a bit empty, as if, having realized my most extravagant ambition by getting Shaharah to sing one of my songs, I was devoid of further ambition. It almost felt too easy. She came in with no preparation and created a thing of effortless charm. Brimming with pride, I sent Morey the latest temp mix of the song. His reply landed like a small explosive device.

> Ok, I really have to be honest about this one so please only take this as constructive criticism which is only my uninformed and biased opinion...

> First the good news—I like the groove, the drums, the overall feel and especially the background soulful vocals, but I really don't like the lead vocal. It's too "polite," has no real soulful rawness to it, it sounds almost like it's not in her comfort zone, like it's in the wrong key for her—it sounds too low, has very

little emotional impact. That's just the way I hear
it...I think she should try to sing at least the chorus
an octave higher, giving it a bit of grit and a rougher,
strained, and yearning edge...even the verses sound
too laid back for me.

How could that be? Either Morey was mistaken or I was.
Shaharah's vocals sounded so wonderfully plush to me. It's
true that the song's key was not in her sweet spot—she'd
mentioned that. And she delivered a decidedly low-key
approach. It's all a matter of personal taste. Still, Morey had
so many notches in his music belt. How could his instincts
be so off? Or if they weren't, then how could *my* instincts
be so off? And if I was so wrong about this song, maybe I
was similarly self-deceived about all my songs and the entire
project was nothing more than ridiculous hubris.

Then the clincher rolled in. Jo's email.

Shaharah is wasted here. I'm disappointed she didn't
alter the melody to better suit her range, like I did
for "Country" and "Basement."

She clearly has a dynamite and powerful voice
but it's not shining through here.

If you could convince her to come in again and
just take a shot singing the song in a way that respects
the underlying melody but also allows her to sing in
her comfort zone, I think it would be magic.

Maybe send her your and my version of "Country" and "Basement" to show her it's ok to take a
little liberty...I also struggled with the melodies and
phrasing and had to wrestle them into something

similar but better suited to my voice. Maybe she was too shy bc she doesn't know you, but encourage her to sing a little outside the box / not stick so faithfully to the line you laid down.

Gonna listen a few more times to pay more attention to other tracks.

And so the beat went on. Shaharah herself emailed later that she thought her voice came out "nicer" than she expected in the low register. And that it's a "great song." But even she suggested adding some pop/R&B-style variations on the melodies in the verses. I replied that I'd certainly be more than happy to take another stab at it.

Further complicating matters, Jo sent another opinion:

Hey...I know u hate it when I say this but...I still think this is a male vocalist's song. Lyrics and low key...and it would sound great with female backups.

I don't think this was the right song for Shaharah. But I would urge her to come back and try "Go Slow" or "Grace"...something that will give her vocal chops a little more room to breathe.

This male/female notion kept coming up with Jo. I asked her to elaborate and she replied in a detailed email:

I can think of a couple of songwriters that I believe write (mostly) male melodies—Dylan, Springsteen...I guess songs that are much more about the words than the melody, or melodies that don't move too much. "Another Man's Crime," to me, is not meant to be sung by a woman. I can see a male vocalist delivering a very cool performance, but a female vocalist has nowhere to go, it will sound flat— it does not give her any place to emote, there is no range in the melody, nor should there be, it would sound over the top. Male vocalists can get away with singing conversationally. Female vocalists need to sing with more emotion, which means more complex melodies with greater range to give them the space to interpret the song.

Does this make any sense?

Like I said, it's an instinct more than anything else. I can see Lou Reed singing "Another's Man's Crime" no problem and it would be great. Joni Mitchell? Not so much. One would be cool, the other plain boring.

I had my doubts about that gender divide. But the more I listened to the recording, the more I heard what Morey and Jo were saying— "Another Man's Crime" was almost there, but not quite.

IT HAD BEEN a month since Morey and I last grabbed a coffee, and I was overdue to consult with my unofficial mentor. We met at a newly opened café on Sherbrooke Street with nautical-themed decor and comfortable club chairs. Morey regaled me with stories about the record biz. The time he played guitar on the demo of a comely teenager who had a rich father and couldn't sing to save her life but went on to become a star on *Beverly Hills 90210*. How her album sold very well, infuriating the songwriter they'd worked with because he'd been paid precious little. "And all I got out of it," Morey said, "was a slice of pizza and a Dr Pepper!" Then there was the guy who bought his song back for one hundred dollars from a record company that was doing nothing with it, only to see it placed in a soap opera with *ka-ching!* results. Or the time Morey's band, the Game, noticed a star producer in the front row at a gig in Quebec City and changed their set list to include a handful of originals. The producer came to the dressing room post-show, inebriated, talking up a storm about how after he finished his current star project, he was going to record the band. They never heard from him again.

Over our usual coffees, we chatted about youth culture as Morey glimpsed it through his daughter's circle of friends. A girl who posted an attractive pic of herself on Facebook would typically receive way more "likes" than when Hayley posted a fantastic song she'd been working on for a week. I had trouble imagining how anyone could be less than impressed with the father-daughter productions, which lately had covered R.E.M., Bob Marley, and Damien Rice, as well as Hayley's beloved Radiohead.

"Keep on track," Morey advised me. "If I criticized Shaharah's lead vocals, it's only because I think the song is actually working well." Ironically, he viewed the issue of lead vocals as something of "a detail"—important, of course, but in fact less critical than the "bed" of the song (the foundation made up of bass, drums, and rhythm guitar), which he liked.

"If I felt you were just some accountant who wanted to record your songs and they had no potential," he said, "I would never have criticized the song the way I did."

He noted that until recently I'd been alone with my acoustic guitar and voice—a limited solo situation unless you're one in a billion. Now I was trying to build on the tunes. Morey said keep at it. "Another Man's Crime" proved the songs would become greater than their original permutations.

The take-home was that I should push every button. Krantzberg. Bilerman. Morey. Get that multi-effects pedal for my guitar to help dream up new soundscapes. The songs you least expect to become something will blossom. Favourites will bomb. Styles will shape-shift. You can never guess which one, or how. Most songs have a kernel that is worthy, that someone like Morey at any rate can pull out of the wreckage and salvage.

The moment was right, said my mentor, to flesh out my songs, deepen the tunes, take chances.

PERFECT SHELL

I WAS TURNING THE corner at a donut shop and gazing up at a drab grey five-storey building as a streetcar clanged by. I was about five hundred kilometres from home, in Toronto, on my way to visit an old singer friend.

I hadn't seen Rebecca Campbell for a good decade since I last caught her performing at a Montreal club. Long before that, we'd played music together in our university days. Now I was hoping to press her vocals into service. Had Jo agreed to sing all my songs, I would have been perfectly happy, but she felt that only one or two were suitable for her voice. Shaharah was an R&B singer, which would only work for that sort of material, not my usual singer-songwriter fare. My voice was, well, my voice. I needed more singers.

Rebecca buzzed me into the building with a yelp of excitement over the intercom. Inside, she looked the same as ever: a funky, artistic woman with shaggy rooster hair, glowing blue eyes, and a petite dancer's figure.

Her apartment was a minimalist abode—a studio with a kitchenette and a loft bed. There was a junior-sized Stella guitar on a stand, an electric keyboard set up, and an accordion nearby. The decor inside was as novel as the exterior of the building was bland. Innumerable tchotchkes lined the walls, including a tiny globe that lit up. Canned goods with wacky names were immaculately arranged on shelves. In the bathroom, shelves displayed hundreds of tiny hotel-issue bathroom products, souvenirs from Rebecca's days as a self-described "road warrior," when she sang in rock bands on tour.

Rebecca had been the songbird girlfriend of my great pal Daniel Sanger, whom I'd befriended in a Latin American history class at Concordia University. Daniel and Rebecca had lived in the Plateau district, the artistic hub of Montreal, in a small flat on Rue de Bullion near Rue Napoléon. Their apartment was so modest that the bathtub was located in what had once been one of the flat's two closets. They would brush their teeth in the kitchen sink and use a toilet that was in the other closet.

Rebecca's voice made my songs sound good in our university days, but she was going places musically and left town to pursue a career. Over the years, she toured extensively as a backup singer with Jane Siberry, and fronted bands like Fat Man Waving, Three Sheets to the Wind, and Porkbelly Futures, the latter led until his death by Paul Quarrington, the acclaimed novelist and songwriter. By the time I caught up with her, she was only occasionally singing on stage, spending more time producing shows and running the Ratspace rehearsal studio with her longtime boyfriend, Robin.

Her lifestyle is spartan but joyful. Music is the gift life has given her, and she does not regret for a second the material sacrifices it has entailed. Yet on the late afternoon when we met, she was unsure as to what her next musical step in life would be. There was a hint of burnout.

But that was only in terms of her professional, road-warrior nature. Rebecca herself was high-energy, vibrant, and the same beautifully original singer she had always been. This became clear when, after an hour of catching up, we relocated to her kitchen table to try a song. I tuned up her three-quarter-sized Stella guitar and started playing "Perfect Shell," which, having a folkified countryish flavour, I thought might appeal to her. Rebecca put on some over-sized glasses to read the words, and as I sang she pencilled some markings on the lyric sheet, like some medieval nota-tion, to guide her melodically.

The song turned out to be in the wrong key for her, a development I was getting used to. "If you're going to play with female singers, you're going to have to change keys," Rebecca told me. It suddenly dawned on me that Jo, Shaharah, and the other female singers I'd jammed with had all lamented the keys I was asking them to sing in.

I used a capo (a small device clamped on the neck of a guitar) to play the song in a higher key, moving from D major to F major, but the chords sounded tinny, Tiny Tim tinny.

"The chords give a song so much of its flavour," I told Rebecca.

"It's true," she said. "Chords are so important, yet so ineffable."

I gave up on the capo, as it was making the guitar part sound like a ukulele, and transposed the song down to A.

Rebecca could now sing in her comfort zone, staying true to my melody but phrasing with her own rootsy twang, lingering in sweet spots, dipsy-doodling at the end of some lines, like her gorgeous calligraphy, which I remembered well. It was more than I could ever hope for the song.

Later, we tried "Battlefield Mind," my cathartic post-Bach rocking-out song. I figured it would be a good candidate because it was in the key of A, and it indeed sounded like a powerful blues-rock item in her hands.

The songs sprang to life with her vocals. I was elated. "You sounded really great." I said. "Would you be willing to sing these songs in the studio?"

"Sure," she replied. "They're good songs. It would be fun."

Rebecca had plans to be at a dance show and had to be going. I followed her down to the building's basement, where she retrieved her bicycle. A satchel was slung across her chest, bicycle-courier-style. We hugged, the bike between us, and she rode off east along Dundas Street, road warrior still.

THE NEXT DAY, I went to the venue where I first heard the Bach *Cello Suites*, the Royal Conservatory of Music, where a gleaming new concert hall was now joined to the original Victorian building. Inside, I visited the room where I heard Laurence Lesser's glorious rendition of the *Suites*. A sign posted on the door said RECORDING SESSION UNDERWAY, but I didn't hear anything, so I ventured in. Three student types were working on a laptop. I strolled around as if inspecting the venue for my early music orchestra. Or maybe for my laptop ensemble.

Later, at Steve's Music Store on Queen Street West, I tried out a multi-effects pedal that Morey had recommended. But the salesperson could not explain the gadget to me, and it felt tremendously complex, with "stomp" buttons for the foot and toggle switches galore. The pre-set sounds had evocative names. I tried one called "I Can't Explain," wondering if it would give me the loveable guitar sound from that classic by the Who. It was indeed the sound, dialled up.

Your average music store is not a tranquil place. Several guitarists, oblivious to each other, can be counted on to test amps, guitars, and effects pedals with the crunchiest power chords and wickedest licks on their resumés. And most guitarists, for reasons that escape me, tend to employ vast amounts of distortion, or what my pedal was calling "overdrive." Somewhere in the distorted din, I was sure I heard the melody of Bach's "Jesu, Joy of Man's Desiring."

LABYRINTH OF VOICES

BACK HOME, MY ADVISERS seemed to be racing ahead of me. Morey emailed me a song he'd written, an impressively constructed pop item called "Lifeline," sung by Hayley. In an odd role reversal, I offered a few modest suggestions. Soon it was on YouTube. I wondered whether some record company or movie or brand would take notice. My guess was someone, something, would recognize the top-drawer talent there.

Ditto for Jo. She emailed me two of her songs that her old friend Wayne had recorded and produced. Also well-crafted, not as stylish as Morey's production — yet her singing went straight to my pleasure centre. The recordings had a certain amount of generic slickness, but that would only help her commercial cause. I would be surprised if she didn't "make it" in some fashion. If I were in charge of the pop-industrial complex, she would make it big.

That said, I felt a tinge of sadness that she was embarking

on a music project without me. As I texted her: "That key-boardless kid with great promise whose life I walked into a year ago in Starbucks is now a complete artist, ready for prime-time dazzlement." I felt as if I'd walked Jo down the aisle en route to her conquering the outside world. The sensation was bittersweet.

"It's all your fault!!!!" she replied.

Both Morey's and Jo's high-gloss productions hit a raw nerve in me. I began to fear that my songs were inferior. That compared to their lushly layered melodies I was stuck on my relentlessly guitar-driven, hopelessly old-fashioned, static material.

Did I have any business setting foot in a studio?

But I did it again. The Shaharah Sessions, Volume 2. As if on cue, the late-season snowstorm was playing outside Studio K. The Ides of March had come and gone, but the wind had been vicious in a way that made spring feel very far off. Snow brought with it warmer weather and a soft beauty.

Shaharah parked her white car in the driveway that Krantzberg had kindly shovelled. She arrived with a page-boy cut and her usual casual glamour, Krantzberg scurrying to the kitchen to make her a pot of tea. They're both big tea drinkers, and he carried down a pot, covering it with a tea cozy that looked more like a knit cap, in a beige houndstooth pattern.

"Wow," Shaharah said.

"Mariam sewed it," Krantzberg explained. "She also made a matching apron and placemats."

I was anxious to get started on "Another Man's Crime," and finally Shaharah took the mic. The plan was, as I'd put it in an email, to let her R&B hair down a bit more, dig deeper into the song, and try lifting the chorus higher. Her effort a couple of weeks earlier had been flawless, but it sounded too much like me, or at least me with a great voice. My phrasings to the T. We had been the victims of her excellent abilities the first time around; she had learned her part too quickly, too faithfully.

Now we set about putting more Shaharah into the equation. With Krantzberg at the controls, she poured her vocal elixir through the pop shield and into the mic, from which it ran through the XLR cable that fed into Krantzberg's computer, registering as squiggly lines on his monitor. The first verse was good, though still straightforward; the second verse ratcheted up the emotion a notch with a few curlicues added to the phrasing, altering it just a bit here and there and sending a frisson of pleasure down my own spinal cable.

But we ran into a wall on the third verse, where the song was trying to "break down." I suggested she hit some higher notes. We proceeded slowly. She stopped every once in a while to ponder what to do next, putting a forefinger to her chin and looking into space, talented teacher and star pupil in one person. But it was not easy. Krantzberg lent a helping hand—he's good with vocals—plinking some notes on his nearby keyboard to remind her of the possibilities in B-flat major.

Somehow it was becoming overly show-tuney—Broadway in the basement. We took a break. The singer was hungry, so we marched upstairs and ate some vegetable lentil soup Mariam had made. We huddled at the small kitchen table, dazed victims of "Another Man's Crime." Shaharah took calls regarding a stage she needed to rent for a new weekly gig. Krantzberg lamented all the preparations required to perform live at a regular venue. "I don't miss doing that at all," he said. He did it for twenty-five years and had only recently started slowing down.

Then we headed back to the basement studio and made another attempt at the third verse. She sang up and down and back up the scale, rising energetically to a heightened pre-chorus, and improvised some sumptuous, soul-flavoured lines, adding grit, upping the ante before finding her way to the fade-out.

By then we were all pretty spent, and after one more listen we called it a day. Shaharah got in her car and I slung my electric guitar over my shoulder. I walked down to Sherbrooke, and the snow was all confetti and the automobiles were all messed up and I remembered the similar storm three months earlier, when I'd first laid down tracks with Krantzberg.

I felt fulfilled, imagining that we'd really created something, yet also struck by the fact that Shaharah had worked so hard on a song that was legally speaking not hers. It is a tough grind for gifted musicians who don't have hit songs they can call their own. As a songwriter, I felt privileged yet somehow exploitative. There was also the uncomfortable awareness that women have it tougher than men in the music business. It was no accident that the producers, engineers, and instrumentalists I was in touch with were mostly men. The singers I knew tended to be women. For every Celine or Beyoncé there were countless women like Jo, whose talent had never seen the light of day, and Rebecca, a brilliant vocalist often in the shadows singing backup, and Shaharah, working very hard in a crowded field to get to the next level.

The snowfall was turning harsh. Walking was hard. Three months earlier I'd left my guitar at the studio and marvelled at the storm of the half-century, but this time I cut my hike short and hopped on an eastbound bus.

Back home, I could not resist emailing what we'd recorded to Jo, my hardest-to-please critic. Not for the first time, I was deflated by her verdict.

"Much better, looser, you can hear her massive potential when she goes up an octave — but — I don't think writing melodies on the fly is her forte. Sorry . . . she has the goods no doubt, but needs guidance."

"But the melody is my handiwork," I replied. "What are you referring to exactly?"

She texted back that Shaharah's voice demanded a whole new melody line in this key, and where Shaharah had improvised changes, Jo was underwhelmed.

I was crestfallen. It had to be my failure: "Well, I'm to blame for that, I guess. Maybe my hopes for this song are just out of whack with my abilities."

"No!!" Jo texted back. "Jeez . . . It's the wrong key for her! You will work with vocalists who have amazing voices and that's it, and you have to write a melody line that suits them."

After a few more attempts by Jo to reassure me that my songwriting was not — as I suspected she felt deep down — melodically challenged, the subject took a lighter tack.

"Why don't you try male vocalists?" she asked.

I asked her whether my song "Grace of Love" (which I was now wondering about vis à vis Shaharah) should have a male singer as well.

"No, 'Grace' can work with a vagina," she concluded.

When morning came round, I risked more comeuppance by emailing the song to Morey. But to my surprise, he was not all gloom. According to Morey, the song seemed to be moving in a "ballad" direction, whereas before he'd assumed it had R&B aspirations. He agreed that the third verse, where Shaharah took off with high-octane improv, was uneven, but that it made the song interesting. He had a few suggestions that struck me as easily enough implemented. He advised me to layer more instrument texture on the second verse and bolster the energy following the breakdown section.

The song had acquired a new lease on life. All of us— Morey, Jo, Shaharah, Krantzberg, and me—had differing takes on the tune. I had to figure it out based not on consensus or convention, but on my own wild bias.

An article published at the time in *The New Yorker* by the pianist Jeremy Denk, "Every Good Boy Does Fine," chronicled the piano lessons of his boyhood and beyond. Towards the end of the essay, Denk's words resonated for me: "There's a labyrinth of voices inside your head, a counterpoint of self-awareness and the remembered sayings of your guides and mentors, who don't always agree... They have given all the help they can; the only person who can solve the labyrinth of yourself is you."

THIS IS WHAT YOU
SHOULD BE DOING

I WAS HAVING LUNCH with Jo at Le Taj, an Indian spot in the heart of downtown. Lunching with her was more often than not an adventure; there was no telling what would transpire with conversation, libation, or post-prandial excursions. But on this occasion I arrived at the Stanley Street restaurant with an agenda firmly in mind. I had known Jo for more than a year, music had dominated our friendship, yet I had no clue as to how she came to be so musical. She was exerting a heavy influence on my songs—her thumbs-down on a verse, chorus, or bridge, would send any composition of mine into massive reconstruction. I wanted to know what was on her musical curriculum vitae.

"Tell me your story," I said over a bowl of mulligatawny soup. "How did you get started with music?"

"My parents aren't musicians, but they both can carry a tune," Jo told me. "My mother actually has a very lovely voice, but growing up in very rural small-town Italy, they never had opportunities to explore it. It wasn't like, 'You're taking piano lessons.' It was more like, you know, 'Go find an onion down the street!'—that was their goal for the day. And their meal for the week!"

Warming to the subject, she continued: "My father used to sing Puccini arias when he shaved. That was the extent of his musicianship." But he had "typical immigrant" plans that "my daughter is going to be Jane Austen. She's going to play the piano, sew, and cook, and be this well-rounded young woman. They tried." Jo flashed a smile.

The restaurant featured Hindu plaster carvings flagging the buffet table, elaborate wooden carvings on the walls, and a glass wine tower bisecting the room. Jo was working on a bowl of the velvety, flavourful soup, chasing it with a glass of white wine.

She told me that she started on piano at the age of four, taking Yamaha group lessons at a strip mall where the main attraction was the Woolco discount department store. A few years later, her parents hired a private piano teacher.

"Mr. Ferrera started coming to our house every Wednesday night from like five to six," she recalled. "He'd show up and he always looked like a million bucks; he looked like a movie star. He had a suit and tie, his hair was all slicked back, his cologne always smelled great, very charming and smooth—he was like a superstar, giving piano lessons in some kid's basement. It's like if someone had sent my dad to charm school and trained him on how to act as if he was interested in me—that was Mr. Ferrera."

Although Mr. Ferrera subjected Jo to the heavy lifting of endless piano scales and difficult Bach études, she became very attached to him. "I loved him," she said. "One day he showed up and sat down on the bench next to me and said, 'Well, this is going to be our last lesson. I've taken you as far as I can take you. Here's the name and number of my colleague, he can take you to the next level.' I spent the next hour with this huge lump in my throat, fighting back tears, doing my scales and arpeggios. Like, how could you do this to me! I felt utterly betrayed and abandoned."

Her new teacher turned out to be very strict and old-school. She felt zero personal connection with him and dreaded the lessons. As soon as her parents' car reached Decarie Boulevard, where the teacher lived, panic would set in. "I hated it. And it made me start to hate piano. I wanted to quit. But he fired me before I got a chance to quit."

What he did was suggest Jo start with a new teacher. At thirteen, a pupil at the Villa Maria private school, she rode the subway downtown in her kilt and itchy green knee socks and huge glasses. From the subway she walked to McGill University's massive grey stone music building and up the steps beneath the imposing statue of Queen Victoria.

She felt beaten down by two teachers. Waiting for her was her third, Ross Caulfield, who greeted her with a warm hug. "It was like love at first sight. He was a wonderful, wonderful man and he got me. He saw that I was never going to be a concert pianist, but he saw something in me and decided he was going to let me run with it, provide me with a little bit of guidance, but not crush it."

We made another trip to the buffet table, which was crowded with downtown office workers on their lunch breaks, and returned with plates of tandoori chicken, curried eggplant, and rice.

Jo resumed her story. With her new teacher, she embarked on a conservatory training that lasted seven years. Along the way, Caulfield was privy to her various high school phases. "I went from nerd to rocker to goth. All the stages. He was there. He saw my getups changing, my eyeliner thickening and lessening again, my hair being teased and unteased, bangs, no bangs, glasses, contact lenses, my skirt being rolled up, unrolled — he saw me go through it all.

"He taught me to appreciate classical music. But at heart I just loved to compose pop music. I was locked in my room listening to Top 40."

Jo's singing voice, to my surprise, didn't play a prominent role in her musical past. She sang the songs she wrote — but in private. "I didn't have the confidence," she said.

She finished her conservatory program, and that was that. Then: "Young adulthood. I got distracted. Went to university. Music became like a nice part of my past, but I didn't pursue it. I didn't know what to do with it."

Jo married, moved to the suburbs, went to work with her husband in the financial services sector, and gave birth to a son. A few years before I met her, she divorced, moved back to the city, and started a new career as a real estate agent.

We finished off our heaping plates and made another trip to the buffet table, this time for almond pistachio rolls. A waiter brought coffee. Digging into dessert, Jo said that a decade earlier she had thought of taking lessons again. "Whenever I start feeling completely empty in my life, music is my lifeline," she said. She repeatedly tried to call Mr. Caulfield, only to learn that he had died.

"He's this constant voice in my head, that little angel

on my shoulder, saying, 'Do it. This is what you should be doing!'"

ZOOM

I BECAME THE PROUD owner of a device. And it was such an impressive device that I felt as if I'd joined a band. It was a multi-effects pedal and went by the name of Zoom G3.

The other pedals I'd tested out had more firepower than I needed, ranging in sizes from a paperback novel to a toaster oven, with dozens of distortion effects alone, and knobs to further tweak the sound parameters. One of them, as advertised on YouTube, promised "pretty well the entire history of rock 'n' roll amplifiers in one unit."

When Morey recommended the Zoom, I googled the thing, which meant that on YouTube I got to hear anonymous guitarists wail away with monster amounts of distortion. Zoom seemed to have the right combo of pre-set sounds and tweaking possibilities, as well as a built-in drum machine. At less than two hundred dollars, it was a relative bargain.

So Zoom G3 it was. We hit it off, Zoom and me. I spent the better part of the weekend connected to my electric guitar, which was itself connected to the gadget, producing a smorgasbord of sounds from angelic to demonic. Some of the pre-set sounds, or "patches" as I learned they are called, have evocative names, such as Squeak, Z Scream, Bomber ("produces an explosive sound when picking"), and ExtremeDS ("boasts the highest gain in the world"). "Gain" or "drive" seemed to refer in neutral terms to very distorted sounds that I generally stayed clear of. Simply stepping on the stomp button to activate those sounds would often produce a malevolent hum coming through the amp before I so much as touched my guitar, a hint I would take to quickly move on to a more benign effect like, ModDelay or the Vibe.

The distortion effect, so ubiquitous in rock music, came into the world by accident. In 1951, Ike Turner was on his way to Memphis when his amplifier fell out of the car and broke. At Sam Phillips's Sun Studio, Turner plugged his guitar into the amp and distorted sound came out. Phillips liked the dirty sound. What was arguably rock 'n' roll's very first recording, "Rocket 88," was the result.

The sound was here to stay. "Let's face it," declared a special edition of *Computer Music* magazine in 2013, "we like distortion. We like raw, rough, crunchy sounds that spit and growl."

As well as crunchy sounds and umpteen other cleaner effects, my Zoom had a decent little drummer inside. By activating the drum machine, selecting the tempo and some limited drum patterns, I felt as if I was playing in a combo, and with a wide palette of *Star Wars*-y sounds for my guitar—flangers, delays, echoes, phasers, choruses.

I was deliriously happy and texted Jo, boasting that I'd bought an effects pedal—"no more hopelessly old-fashioned acoustic granola kumbaya chords for me!"

"Congrats!" she replied. "You played with it yet?"

"It's up and running, a fun toy with a learning curve and compositional potential." Later I added: "Just figured out an adjustable drum machine in the gizmo. Kid in candystore-ing. What a gas—suddenly I'm playing in a trio all by myself."

"Every man's dream come true," she retorted, "a three-some with no commitment and u didn't even have to buy dinner."

The plan was to use Zoom as a compositional and arran-ging device. I'd try writing new songs, as well as layering my current songs with a vastly expanded palette of guitar sounds. The drum machine in the device would also help kick-start new ideas. This I started to do with Shaharah in mind.

I'd asked Shaharah whether she was interested in trying a couple of other songs. We made plans and she came over after her gym session. I showed her an array of raw teas, and she took some time gauging their aromas before deciding on a mix of two. I also brought out some cookies, which she enjoyed, though she claimed she shouldn't be eating them since she was getting in shape for an upcoming video to go with her new song, "Tonight I'm Letting Go."

I set up Zoom, got a drum track going, and we tried a song I'd recently revamped, "Sign of Design." The key wasn't right for her, so I transposed it down from D minor to A-flat minor. The drum machine started to feel coldly mechanical after a while, and my relentless verse-chorus-verse-chorus on electric guitar wore thin. But Shaharah sounded lovely, giving the song a funk factor that the chords cried out for.

She wanted to know what the lyrics were about. This was a good question. The song's original title was "Sign of Intelligent Design," and it addressed on one hand the controversy over teaching creationism (intelligent design) that had raged some years ago, and on the other hand a freelance writing phase in which I'd reported on design issues for a glossy magazine. I knew nothing about granite countertops, but a friend was a senior editor at the magazine and she managed to get me a number of plum assignments to California and elsewhere. I quickly tried to get up to speed on home design and master the lingo. Raw material for the song resulted. But the word "intelligent" made the chorus too long, so it became just "Sign of Design." In any case, I was trying to fuse the obsession with design — as seen in the only magazines that make a ton of money these days (so-called "shelter" magazines) — with the question of Why the World Exists.

"So the lyrics," I said, "question, um, both marble backsplashes and the meaning of life."

We recorded it on my phone and went to the next tune I had in mind, the latest incarnation of "Grace of Love." This we could keep in its original key, and she gave the melody a lustrous makeover. To watch Shaharah sing is to watch every melodic, harmonic, and rhythmic fibre in her poured into the song; her face mirrors that outpouring, and it's sufficiently mesmerizing that the listener can sometimes be unaware of precisely what's happening to the music.

Another tune done and dusted, stored away in the indispensable smartphone, and probably in need of some variety and edge. Maybe my Zoom assistant would eventually help the cause.

As we paused for some blackberries and almonds, I thought of Morey's reaction when he first checked out Shaharah's website: "She's the total package." He was right. Beautiful, talented, photogenic, well-spoken, with athletic energy, charismatic stage presence, and more. So it was a surprise when Shaharah told me that from a young age she'd battled a serious health problem, a femur bone deficiency. She spent a great deal of her childhood at the Shriners Hospital for Children. "The worst time was between the ages of seven and sixteen," she said. There were many procedures, and she spent as long as one entire year in hospital.

"Music really helped me to deal with the situation, because obviously there were tough times, right?" she told me. "Like, it was painful. It was hard sometimes, you know, being different, not being able to do regular things. I couldn't wear regular shoes, I couldn't do sports, I couldn't wear shorts. I didn't like being different, and some of the procedures I went through were very painful. Music brought me back to a place that was positive."

Performing live — as she'd been doing for eight years, fronting her band, Soulvation — gave her the most musical pleasure. But it wasn't the easiest career path.

"What's the best thing that can happen?" I asked her. "I'm not sure that signing a deal with a record label is the ultimate goal anymore. What's the Holy Grail for a musician like yourself?"

"The best-case scenario is a hit song," she replied. "That's the best thing that can happen to you."

I suggested we try to compose a song together. I'd been tinkering for several days with an idea for her. I gave her the lyrics I'd written for Jo's "Unstoppable," the lyrics I'd worked so hard to craft only to have Jo come up with her own words. This would be sweet revenge. A Top 40 megahit featuring Shaharah and the lyrics Jo had rejected!

I switched the drum machine on at a tempo I'd pinpointed earlier and started vamping on D9 and A minor chords. Shaharah deftly ad-libbed her way through the lyrics, and for about one minute it sounded like the start of an unstoppably solid pop tune. Then the spontaneous composition degenerated on account of my helter-skelter chordplay, my attempt to somehow compose the embryonic song while it was taking its first baby steps. We didn't get beyond that initial groove, but *ahhh* did that initial groove work well! A solid funk foundation had been built.

We had done four songs — two old, one new, one rejected. (She didn't like a composition in progress called "House of Mysteries" very much. Nobody but me seemed to.)

"So what's the next step?" she asked before leaving.

"Eventually we'll go back into the studio," I said.

I wasn't sure which studio. My sessions with Bilerman at Hotel2Tango were coming up in a few weeks. And what about a backing band? And which songs were working best?

The next day, I emailed Jo the Shaharah effort on "Sign of Design." She gave it a thumbs-up.

Vocals sound great, you make a great team. Get some real musicians pronto! Dealing with a personal crisis so can't give you my usual copious notes, but I think it's safe to say you've found your R&B muse :).

That sounded good, but the personal crisis part alarmed

me. And I hoped she wasn't just eager to fob off some other singer on me; she was being uncharacteristically, almost suspiciously, enthusiastic. I offered help on her crisis but she declined, saying that unfortunately there was nothing I could do to help. I was worried about her.

BUILDING A BIGGER BETTER GREATER CHORUS

MOREY WAS WEARING A sheepskin jacket appropriate for the fickle weather. It was the first week of April, but we could not imagine meeting at an outdoor *terrasse* any time soon. We were indoors, at the newly opened café with the vaguely nautical design theme.

Morey said he was intrigued by my musical efforts. He'd heard "Another Man's Crime" morph from a strum-along tune to its current incarnation as a Shaharah-powered R&B wannabe.

"Let me ask you a question," he said. "Do you see yourself as a songwriter, an artist, or a performer?"

"I have no idea," I said. "I've always written songs, so I suppose that makes me a songwriter."

"So would you be happy to just give someone one of your songs—say, Shaharah—and have her and her band do whatever they wanted with it?"

"I'd be honoured," I said.

"And what if someone were to change your song?"

"I wouldn't be overjoyed with a death metal makeover. But the possibility seems very remote." I was labouring over these songs, tinkering under the hood, trying to get them in running order. Being sold for scrap might be all they were good for. The notion of someone else wanting to get behind the wheel seemed unlikely.

Morey, a self-described "control freak," had a different approach to songs. He always saw the entire canvas spread before him, all the instrumental colours and nuances, and always had, ever since he was a kid. He would remember a squeak on a guitar string from measure thirty-two of a Dylan song but not necessarily remember the words of the chorus. He couldn't conceive of a song unless it was a big-picture version with all the tones of the palette, from kick drum to backing vocals. "I'm the opposite of you in that way," he said. "You write a song on guitar, finish the progression and lyrics, and move on to the next one."

Morey said that when he gave one of my songs a listen, he focused on its potential. But I doubted that I could make my songs as successful as the versions that flickered across his auditory imagination. Whenever he suggested that a catchier chorus could be added to a song to make it flourish, I tried it, but with mixed results.

The latest developments in sound recording technology were a godsend for Morey. Now he could realize his panoramic musical vision on a laptop. All the sounds were available, good ones, if he put his mind and time into it. Yet it was highly labour-intensive.

"That's why I'm very careful about what new song I take

on," he said. "It's a huge piece of work. It takes me forever."

Morey's eyes flashed with recognition as his wife and daughter walked into the café. I said hello—we'd met once before, though Hayley was very familiar now from all her YouTube videos. I asked her how she liked the latest father-daughter creation that would be uploaded on YouTube that evening, a glorious account of "Teardrop" by Massive Attack. She liked it. As did I. Morey had been venturing into "trip-hop" territory, and he had a natural talent for the style.

Morey piped up, telling me Hayley was impressed that I'd once interviewed Jonny Greenwood, the Radiohead guitarist. Her big eyes lit up, and I said I could try to find a copy of the article if she was curious.

That evening, Morey gave a listen to the tunes I had recorded on my phone with Shaharah. I imagined him up in his attic studio, surrounded by handcrafted guitars leaning on their stands. Listening on headphones, he probably winced at some of my wonky guitar work and the down-and-dirty iPhone recording. Yet he liked Shaharah's vocals—she was more in her "wheelhouse" on these songs. But he suggested I write bigger choruses for both "Sign of Design" and "Grace"—"onwards and upwards to greater heights," as he put it. As for "Unstoppable," that quickie confection Shaharah and I collaborated on, he thought it worked just fine as a groove. No stadium-sized anthemic chorus required.

So I began racking my brains, trying to graft a new chorus onto "Grace." I came up with two versions but didn't think they improved matters. Frankly, it was hell to revisit the construction of the song once again and try to pluck a new chorus out of thin air. I saw what Morey meant about the pre-chorus wanting to lead to something more substantial than just a glorified verse intoning "There but by the grace of love." What could I do? It was onerous. Another example of my having to live with my limitations.

I was not Morey. I was not Jo.

But I was sensitive to their verdicts. Morey even offered a meta-critique that cut to the bone:

> I think there is a tendency in your songs that they start off well, in that the verses are usually subdued and easy to follow, then they hit a "lift" in a pre-chorus or chorus in a logical place and right where they should, but tend to come back down somewhere in the chorus rather than reach a climax — again, just my opinion of course but the trajectory between verse and chorus, while well intentioned, almost seems unfinished in that they build well and change gears in a good way, but they revert back to the first gear either in the chorus itself or when the verse comes back which loses some of the lift it's already gained... hard to describe, I hope you see what I mean, maybe it's just something I need to explain in person — and you may not agree.

I got his point. And I spent the better part of the weekend trying to construct a bigger better greater chorus for "Grace." I had a number of ideas, all variations on a similar theme, but I ended up rejecting them all. I was a few inches from emailing one or two ideas to Morey or Jo, but I never reached the point where I liked a new chorus enough. I was once again banging my head against the tabula rasa.

SHAHARAH CAME OVER for another jam, this time to work mostly on the new tune, "Unstoppable." She arrived late, toting a salad, which she ate in my kitchen. She was delayed because the owner of a clothing shop spotted her in the takeout joint, recognized her, and insisted upon giving the up-and-coming singer a shirt. It was a grey item declaring LOVE, and she was wearing it atop grey exercise stretch pants and Nike shoes boasting fluorescent orange laces.

After lunch I made her some green tea and she applied some lip balm. We then went into the living room, where I had my electric guitar, Zoom pedal, and small amp set up. I gave her the lyric sheet and started playing the two-chord vamp that constitutes "Unstoppable."

After one run-through, Shaharah placed the lyric sheet on a table and said, "It doesn't feel like a song yet. It feels like half a song."

I got her drift. The song had a perfectly good groove but was spinning its wheels without going anywhere. An idea suddenly came to mind. "Here's a thought. How about you sing just the word *unstoppable*. Stretch the word out. Elongate it. I'll try playing this" —I stroked some bar chords higher up the neck, double-time — "and it could be the chorus."

The notion seemed to work. It gave off a fizzy cocktail vibe and lifted the song out of its two-chord James Brown formula.

"That was great. Doesn't it feel like a song now?" I asked.

"Yes, I think so."

"We're on to something."

I then tinkered with the other lyrics so they fit her phrasing, and we wrote a simple bridge, based on something that had surfaced in our previous jam. We recorded it.

It was progress—quickly thrown together, but progress all the same.

Next we tackled "Sign of Design." I asked Shaharah to improvise with the words "Intelligent Design" while I vamped over two chords to give the song another dimension, a bridge. We were running out of time. We hurriedly recorded it on the smartphone, and then she had to run off to meet a friend. Someone had given her tickets to the Alicia Keys concert.

"People are always giving you stuff," I said.

I felt as if I'd just given her a hit song.

ARE WE IN FUNKYTOWN YET?

WHEN I ASKED KRANTZBERG if he knew of a keyboard player who could play something soulful for "Another Man's Crime," he suggested Steve Corber. Hoping to add some texture and lift to the song, I hired him.

We arrived at Krantzberg's home at the same time. Lean, balding, and bespectacled, Corber was identifiable by his briefcase, which was emblazoned with the black and white keys of a piano. Although it was early April, fat, lazy snowflakes fell, mocking the calendar. They wouldn't last, but Krantzberg had managed to summon up snow for a session yet again.

Corber was a classically trained pianist who had experience with jazz and pop as well. Interestingly, he was also a teacher of Transcendental Meditation (TM).

TM, he posted on a Facebook discussion, is "the process of opening our awareness to that area of silence and calm and peace that we locate deep within each of us at the source of thought, an unbounded field of creative intelligence."

The TM technique, he continued, strengthens the thought process, making it "clear and sharp and the musical ideas unfold effortlessly."

I hoped that would be the case for us in the basement studio. "Another Man's Crime" was nearly complete, with two rhythm guitars, bass, drums, Shaharah's lead vocals, Jo's harmonies, and an electric guitar solo. Morey had advised me to bring another instrument into the song after the first chorus to add a new dimension. Ergo Corber.

We soon went to work, with Corber playing Krantzberg's MIDI controller keyboard. The sound was set to a Rhodes electric piano. But the effect was overly celestial and too much on the higher register of the piano. I started to back-seat drive what Corber was doing. We kept at it, Krantzberg engineering, Corber playing, me making constant suggestions.

They were both seated before the computer. I was standing behind them, peering over two small bald spots amid thinning hair and glimpsing their own points of view through the sides of their glasses. I felt like a kid in the back of a station wagon on a family road trip.

Are we in Funkytown yet?

We were not.

Every time I asked Corber to redo a section he'd recorded, he would simply get Krantzberg to make the change on the computer. Because Corber was playing a MIDI controller, the sounds he was producing were all digital data. Meaning they could be modified in the computer. A graphic display of Corber's performance was pictured on the monitor. When, for example, I found the voicing of one chord too high, Corber would ask Krantzberg to move the cursor over to the musical staff on the screen. Krantzberg would then drag the uppermost note in a chord down an octave on the staff. The chord voicing was thereby altered graphically and as a result musically.

I found this both amazing and disconcerting. No longer in a recording studio, I was in a software lab. When a part was slightly off rhythmically, they'd fix the timing the same way.

"Let's quantize that," Corber would say about a particular note. This was like Auto-Tune for rhythm, enabling each note to fall precisely on the beat. "Let's see the grid," he would then say. Krantzberg would open the visual display of music notation, where every nuance of notes and chords was shown on multicoloured horizontal bars. They'd extend the duration of a chord, bring the placement of two chords closer together, you name it.

"It's like paint-by-numbers," Corber said.

It was like recording in my accountant's office. It brought to mind a podcast in which the famed producer Don Was spoke about how different digital recording is from the old analogue way of doing things. He mused about how quantizing and click tracks differ from the way records were made by bands like the Rolling Stones in the early 1970s.

"If you're making records to a click track...there's a metronome counting exactly where the beats are, or you're doing what a lot of people do now, where you actually do something called quantizing the beat, so 1 is exactly on 1, and if someone doesn't hit the beat on the 1, it moves it over to the nearest beat automatically in digital recording," the producer said in the NPR podcast *All Things Considered*.

"So when everything is quantized like that, if you want to play in that musical universe it's akin to diving off a diving board into a little flute of champagne—you've got to land in that specific area or you sound really out of rhythm, and it sounds really goofy and sloppy and messy. The beauty of the Rolling Stones is that because each of these five guys feels the beat in a little different place and no one's correcting it—if you want to play along with them it's like diving into a lake and you've got all this room from where the beat lives."

At Studio K., when it came to adding piano, Corber and Krantzberg were diving into a little flute of champagne.

Time and again, I'd suggest Corber change something in his performance, and he'd then try to make the fix on the computer by tinkering with a parameter like "velocity."

"Can't we actually replay this line?" I'd say. "There was another section that seemed slightly off." Corber was affable and would agree, but often he'd shrug, as if I was asking him to reinvent a wheel that was already in the computer.

The minutes went by, as did another billable hour. Corber seemed to be playing more of a detached style, staccato as opposed to legato. I preferred the more fluid legato, with each note blending and blurring into its neighbours. Perhaps he was playing in a detached way so that the notes could be more perfectly manipulated in the computer. From where I stood, I was actually seeing his keyboard by peering through his glasses. I wasn't sure about his musical point of view. It was dizzying.

Mariam came down to the basement to say hi to Corber. She was wearing a fedora and a trench coat. She looked like a detective. "I'm going to meet someone for a drink," she said.

She left, and we finished up the track in a rush. Corber

had to be at a ballet practice for children, where he had a regular gig playing piano. I hoped the kids were not dancing to a quantized beat.

HOW "UNSTOPPABLE"
BECAME "INFLAMMABLE"

Jo FINALLY CAME UP for air. She wanted to meet for lunch, but not at the salad joint where I was already installed. "I need a Bloody Caesar," she texted.

I agreed to swing by the Claremont for a coffee. Her "personal crisis," as it turned out, was two things: a friend in desperate need, and what she described as "man trouble." But she was her usual effervescent self. Regardless of whatever personal Sturm und Drang Jo might be going through, she was remarkably upbeat whenever we met up in person. In this way, she embodied her two (usually hidden) tattoos. One consisted of the Chinese characters for "seize the moment." The other, which she got later in life, was Chinese for "endurance." She subsisted on the two philosophies.

As we worked on our respective beverages, we compared notes on music. I mentioned a storied Nashville studio I'd read about that spits out CDs an hour or two after a recording session. She was keen to go.

Jo had become enraptured by the process of recording her own songs. Her sessions tended to be late-night weekend marathons that featured a certain amount of merriment. The results that I'd heard via email were impressively polished.

For my part, I played her an excerpt from my "Unstoppable" jam with Shaharah, complete with the lyrics I'd originally penned for Jo's song of the same name. Her face crinkled and she said, "Those are my words!"

I shrugged. "You refused them for your song." She listened some more and made a sour face. I took the phone away.

"Just an idea," I said.

"Shaharah sounds good," she conceded.

A few days later, I emailed her that recording. Her response threw me: "You cannot call your song 'Unstoppable' or make that the theme of the song. I will be royally pissed."

What? The song that had such promising momentum was suddenly immobilized. Would she really insist on intellectual property rights for the word *unstoppable*? That's all I'd taken from her song—one word. How much credit can anyone claim for a single word? A generic and hackneyed word at that. More to the point, she'd asked me to write lyrics for her song, and when I produced them she took a pass. Twenty-four hours after her request, she'd already written her own words. She liked my lyrics, so she said; they suited her, but the phrasing wasn't perfect—I was supposed to believe that one day she would use them for something else. The world wasn't big enough for two "Unstoppables," but her individual repertoire was?

And could a song title be copyright-protected anyway? I didn't think so. I could write a song called "My Way," and nobody would sue.

A quick Internet search revealed no shortage of songs called "Unstoppable," including those by Public Enemy, Christina Aguilera, Lil Wayne, Kat DeLuna, E. S. Posthumus (a group that bases its compositions on Pythagorean philosophy), and a girl in a blue-and-white striped shirt looking to be about eight years old and belting it out on YouTube.

Jo clearly had not cornered the market with this theme. But my research was counting for little with a songwriter who felt hard done by.

"Not listening," she replied when I texted her later. "Too pissed."

"The words were quickly tossed into a new melody," I explained. "They're mostly temporary."

Jo was not happy. "If you had a colleague read a draft of your new book and asked for their opinion and then they sent you a draft of *their* new book and it had the same title and theme but said it was only temporary so don't worry, would you be pissed? So ya, I'm serious. Until words and title are different I've no inclination to listen. I think it's incredible you think I'd feel otherwise!"

A full-blown contretemps was underway.

I wrote back: "Given the genesis of those lyrics I'm assuming you don't truly think I'm secretly poaching your ideas (as your analogy suggests)."

No reply. Now I was miffed, though at the same time I could see how maybe her nose was out of joint. I tried to imagine how I would feel if she sent me a song of her own that happened to be called "Go Slow" or "Basement Rainbow." I sort of empathized. In a huff, I speedily rewrote lyrics for the entire song. They were much better lyrics, I felt. I had her in mind somewhat.

The new title: "Inflammable."

The next day I sent my peace offering. "Your cease-and-desist order lit a fire under my song," I texted. "Lyrics and theme totally rewritten—not quite finished, but there will be no more unlawful use of your copyright. I'm sorry if I upset you."

She texted back her thanks, which I was relieved to see. I had feared her flammable nature might spell the end of our friendship.

"I hope you can understand why it did not sit right with me," she said. "Thanks for respecting my request."

"All I can say," I texted back, "is if you ever get a hankering to write a song called 'Papyrus' you'll be plain outta luck."

"I think we're good," she said.

SPRING WAS FINALLY in the air after the cruellest extension of winter in recent memory. Massive piles of snow, dumped by city cleanup crews, sat in parks like sad monuments. Hockey boards were taken down. It had been a long haul, but the segue in Montreal from Cold City to Hot City is an overnight sensation.

I was hunkered down in a basement studio, trying to turn a folk song into something steamier.

It began with an email from Krantzberg titled, "Just

messing around." Concerned that his keyboardist friend had not quite provided the funkification I'd wanted for "Another Man's Crime," Krantzberg had created an audacious remix of the song, with a techno-type drum loop and some keyboard stabs of his own.

I liked the idea and had visions of a trip-hop account that would do justice to Shaharah. Maybe this was the answer to the song's woes. It seemed like a quixotic undertaking, but it also seemed to be working, in a perverse kind of way. Using Krantzberg's foundation as a starting point, we added clubland beats, a minimalist bass, and tossed in some keyboards. With Shaharah's voice added, we left it to marinate.

"This could be a flash in the pan," I said. "I have no idea what it will sound like tomorrow."

Mariam knocked on the sliding door and came in with a batch of mail: Krantzberg's monthly newsletter from the musicians' union and a gaggle of wedding RSVPs. They were getting married in a month's time. I had a feeling the new clubby mix we'd cooked up wouldn't be around by the time they tied the knot.

PRELUDE2HOTEL2TANGO

IT WAS LATE APRIL. Income tax returns were in the mail. The Montreal Canadiens were in the playoffs. I was in a tunnel of tunes, and the light at the other end was Bilerman's studio, where three sessions were booked, starting in a few days.

With me at the Hotel2Tango studio would be Bilerman at the engineering controls and a hired-gun rhythm section, Morgan Moore on bass and Bucky Wheaton on drums.

Bilerman had recommended Morgan and Bucky, said they played well together. To do a bit of advance planning, I met up with Morgan at his flat, located above an Indian restaurant on St. Laurent Boulevard, the street that divides east from west, and to a large extent English from French, in the city.

Morgan Moore doesn't conform to easy stereotypes. His website shows him in crisp white shirt collars, bent over a stand-up bass, and mentions that he's an avid golfer. But when I arrived, he looked every inch the rumpled artist. He had a just-rolled-out-of-bed look; his wavy brown hair had apparently not seen a brush for some time.

Morgan's specialty is jazz. But he can play anything— roots music as well as the sort of alternative edgy material that his girlfriend composes for her band, Blood and Glass. Her CD, which he gave me, sounds a bit like Björk. I like Björk because I once interviewed her on the phone and all we discussed was the dream in her head when she woke up that morning.

We took seats around a blond wood coffee table as the afternoon sun broke through heavy clouds and tumbled through his salon window. I noted a Milan Kundera novel, a sunburst Fender Jazz Bass, and framed photos of jazz greats.

If Morgan looked tired, it was probably because he had very recently returned from a trip to India, where he'd given jazz workshops and travelled around and fallen head over heels for the subcontinent. He told me how he was struck by the contrast in India "between peacefulness and explosiveness, between chaos and order." He showed me an iPhone app for Indian music rhythms that he was keen on using as a practice aid.

After some enjoyable small talk, I removed my acoustic from its case and Morgan grabbed his Fender. I gave him the chord charts I'd written out for some songs. (Without the benefit of a formal musical education, writing out those charts was an ambitious exercise in musical literacy.) He leaned back on his couch and found his way easily through each number, altering his basslines as he went, testing various waters. It all sounded splendid to me, but that's generally the case when I jam and sing with a top-flight musician. I'd learned to record with my iPhone so that after the fact I could gauge what had really transpired.

After a couple of hours, we put our instruments down and discussed the upcoming sessions.

"Who's the producer going to be?" Morgan asked.

"Good question." I wasn't sure whether Bilerman would play the role of a producer or engineer. An engineer mostly focuses on the technical aspects of a recording session, setting up mics and amps, pushing the buttons, and helping to bring out the best possible version of a performance. It can be crucial to how the music ends up sounding.

A producer is more intimately involved in the big picture of the song and deals with issues like who should be playing, arrangement, performance, and overall vibe. Although Krantzberg had been hands-on, directing backup vocals in one case and showing a very good ear for what was on or off musically, he had been primarily acting as an engineer with me. Meanwhile, Bilerman's credits usually referred to him as having "made" records as opposed to producing or engineering them. I had no idea what his role would be once we got into the studio.

All I knew was that I had four songs that were very close to being finished in Krantzberg's studio. I'd started three other tunes that had problems and might or might not be salvaged. If I could get a handful of songs out of the sessions with Bilerman, I'd have an album's worth of material.

Morgan asked if I'd like to check out the sound of Bucky Wheaton, the drummer who was going to join us at Hotel-2Tango. We listened to a song that featured Bucky's drumming—fairly ordinary, until an interlude in which he shone.

"Tell Bucky he's in," I said. "Though it was touch and go for a while until the interlude."

"Ha!"

I bid Morgan Moore goodbye and couldn't help but think how incredibly affable and good-natured every last musician I'd been in touch with had been. Maybe it went with the territory of pursuing musical dreams.

H2T: SESSION NO. 1

I WAS APPREHENSIVE ABOUT my big moment with Bilerman. It wasn't playing my parts that worried me but the challenge of meshing with strangers on drums and bass and somehow making the songs work. I would be paying more money than I'd ever coughed up for my songs — for studio time and for the rhythm section of Morgan Moore and Bucky Wheaton. We might crank out three songs a day or spend ten hours on one tune. The chemistry might be non-existent. Or we could find ourselves clicking nicely as a trio. Friends were using words like "exciting" and "fun" for the three sessions I'd booked at Hotel2Tango. But the prospect of a debacle was uppermost in my mind.

I pulled my two guitars, electric and acoustic, out of my car and strolled up to the door of the studio a few minutes early. The building is not one of the industrial structures typical of the area but has a modernist feel, as if it had a previous life as a new-agey church.

As I contemplated the architecture that cloudless morning, Howard Bilerman arrived, dressed in black, unlocking and alarm-disabling our way into the studio. Bucky Wheaton showed up soon afterwards carrying a snare drum ("best snare in town," said Bilerman). Tall and lean, he gave the impression of a surfer dude. He was wearing cargo shorts, sandals, and a T-shirt with a caricature of a face that seemed like one I should recognize. He started setting up a kit made up mostly of sparkly red Ludwig drums arrayed on a burgundy oriental rug.

Soon we were joined by Morgan Moore, who was carrying two instruments, a gigantic upright bass and his Fender electric. Morgan and Bucky greeted each other as long-lost pals, hugging with dramatic flair.

Morgan was in a dark T-shirt, dark pants, chunky boots, and soon donned a hoodie. He seemed a bit jumpy and mentioned something about too much caffeine. He set a case on the hardwood floor of the big tracking room and removed the cover, revealing a pirate's chest of multicoloured effects pedals. He plugged in his electric bass and started to warm up.

Before the music-making got underway, Morgan realized he had a problem with one of his fingernails and was missing a key piece of equipment: a nail clipper. So he went off on a shopping expedition. Bucky put in an order for a pack of cigarettes and Bilerman requested some "trail mix that's not too sugary."

Meanwhile, Bilerman was setting me up in the tracking room, near the huge poster of the shapely circus girl and fierce tiger. I was positioned in my own little workstation, about twenty feet from the high-hat side of Bucky's drums and separated by an orange sound baffle. Sitting on a chair, I had my acoustic guitar resting on a stand, two microphones directly in front of me (one for my voice, the other for my guitar), a lyric sheet on a music stand, and headphones attached to a mixer box with several volume knobs. These enabled me to adjust the relative levels of my guitar, my voice, Bucky's drums, and Morgan's bass in my headphones. From the other side of "the glass," inside the control room, Bilerman could hear us and communicate over the "talkback" system. Krantzberg's basement studio felt light years away.

Morgan returned with smokes, trail mix, cashews, and a nail clipper. The instant band was ready to go.

I had chosen "Go Slow" as the first song and gave Morgan and Bucky the chord charts I'd written out. We spent a couple of hours on it, just like a real band, mapping the song out, turning *terra incognita* into familiar territory, searching for the right drum accents and basslines, doing several takes. Then we'd go into the control room to listen with Bilerman, resolving to do something better or differently before heading back into the big room to take another shot at the tune.

Playing guitar and singing into the mic, I could hear the rest of the band crystal clear in the headphone mix and was close enough to make eye contact. Bucky seemed to be into it, eyes sometimes shut, lost in the trance of his own drum pattern, occupying the heart of the tune; Morgan was bopping, occasionally emitting a yelp that indicated either enthusiasm or a mistake.

We worked on the interlude, a recently composed add-on to make the song breathe more. Bucky filled the five-bar section with thunderous drumming, and that part of the song became what I'd hoped—a departure from the relentless guitar-led progression. We were tight. Everything was jelling. There was a crisp jauntiness to the song, powered by a marching beat. I was enamoured with what Morgan and Bucky had played. Here and there Morgan had added a few passing notes that embroidered the tune with understated beauty.

Even my vocals sounded good, though both my voice and guitar playing were temporary "guide tracks," only there to guide the rhythm section. I would have to return to the studio at a later date to properly record my guitar, alongside whoever would be singing.

Lounging on the dark leather couch in Bilerman's control room after a great many run-throughs, we were all happy with the results of the latest take. One song down!

Before we dove into the next song, I mentioned that I'd be getting a "real" singer to sing "Go Slow." Morgan begged to differ. "People want to hear the songwriter's voice," he said. "I understand if you want to re-record your vocals, but you should sing the song." I told him, accurately, that I sing the other songs much worse.

Next tune: "Basement Rainbow," the first song I attempted in Studio K., but with which I was never satisfied. They apparently liked that song as well, Morgan shadowing the guitar hook with ethereal chords. He is not the sort of bass player who sits back and blends into the woodwork of the song, yet he was managing his front-and-centre inclinations with subdued eloquence. Bucky, for his part, created shimmering cymbal statements that sweetly ushered in each verse. Drummer and bassist had set up sturdy scaffolding for the facade of a gentle, relaxed ballad.

We worked well together and crafted—really crafted—the song, sweating it out, playing it maybe two dozen times before it seemed right. We choreographed an ending. *This is what it feels like to be in a band*, I thought. Pretty excellent.

It occurred to me that Bilerman was right about the magic of a live performance. I was skeptical when he first told me about his approach—to capture a band performing well, as if it was nothing simpler than that. The notion that I could join a just-add-water band in the studio and whip up song after song did not strike me as very simple. But here we were, finessing two songs in a row.

The food delivery arrived and we broke for lunch, relocating to the small room that encompassed a kitchenette, espresso machine, table, pinball machine, and little trampoline.

Bilerman had ordered couscous with vegetables, Maghrebian sauce, and grilled chicken breasts. Talk was of cronies Morgan and Bucky played in bands with, rockers misbehaving, getting wasted, a femme fatale singer who broke the hearts of two pals, Morgan getting fired for trashing a hotel room. (Although the worst of the damage seemed to involve a banana splattered on the ceiling, the band got stuck with a hefty cleaning tab.) If I felt like part of the band while playing, over lunch I felt like an outsider as Bucky and Morgan went down memory lane.

Back in the recording (or tracking) room, the next song on my list was "Honey from the Sky." The initial jam had a euphoric quality. Morgan threw in a highly catchy, incandescent bassline. But the song swallowed us. The tempo got overly fast. We lost time with spacey effects from pedals and question marks surrounding the drums. We'd play and play and troop into the control room, plop down on the sofa, and listen to so-so results. Morgan loved the song, but I was fearful that his sugar-coated bass riff would wear thin after a few listens. Back to the big room for a slightly different and, as time went on, faster spin. Eventually Bilerman's soothing voice would pipe into our headphones with the suggestion that we come and give it a listen.

It has been said that when some composers perform an original song, there is an emotional return to the moment of composition. It was often like that for me in the studio. Although I should have been focusing on what the band was playing, my mind often wandered off into the psychological space where the song was first created. For "Honey from the Sky" it was a return to dawn slowly emerging in Montreal on a very cold winter day as I strummed an electric guitar and gazed though a window at the bare trees and rooflines of a sombre city. A feeling and a scene, very much connected to the chords and rhythm of the song.

A callus on Morgan's finger had split open. We watched him apply some Krazy Glue to seal it. As the day wound down, drummer and bassist were both checking their iPhones like mad. Bilerman, meanwhile, was cool and calm in the control room. He only occasionally had suggestions (always good ones), usually when we asked. His presence was stable and reassuring. It made sense that he played goalie in his ball-hockey league.

Bilerman played us back the very first take, and we returned to the basics in a desperate attempt to recapture that lost vibe. By the time we did finish, nobody had the appetite to listen anymore. It was 8 p.m.; we'd been going since 10 a.m. We'd have a version to listen to the next morning.

By this time we were peeking at a live stream of the Canadiens game playing on the computer. Bucky (in a rush to catch the rest of the game) and Morgan flew out of the studio. Bilerman locked up and left a few minutes later, and a woman pulled up in his newly bought black 1980 Fiat Spider roadster.

"Now I look like a producer," he said.

H2T: SESSION NO. 2

I GOT TO HOTEL2TANGO at eleven the next morning, just as Bucky, snare drum in hand, arrived, and we commiserated about the Canadiens' overtime loss.

We buzzed the intercom and one of Bilerman's assistants let us in. Bilerman himself had a dental appointment and was going to be a bit late. Morgan made his appearance, and after a trip to the espresso machine we congregated in the control room, where we listened to the previous session's last take of "Honey from the Sky," that brick wall in the key of A minor which had halted all our good progress. I expressed my doubts about Morgan's catchy neon-lit bass riff, which was driving the thing.

"We can take the song in one of two directions," I said. "As is, or more moody." I wanted it to be more moody.

"Let's put this aside for now and move on to another song," said Bucky.

That seemed like a sensible, diplomatic strategy. I opted

for a song called "Achilles" and gave Morgan and Bucky the chord charts. The song stems from a highfalutin idea: to put the words of Homer's *Iliad* to music. I'd recently read the beginning of Robert Graves's translation of *The Iliad*, and the musicality of the words had struck me. Although his translation is in prose, there are sections he renders in verse. The very start of the epic, removing a few words, formed an obvious melody in my head: *Sing, Mountain Goddess, sing through me / That anger which most ruinously / Inflamed Achilles.*

I kept going till I had some twenty verses, which did not even sum up Book 1 of the epic poem. I slapped a chorus onto it, using my own words, and then came up with another song from the twenty-four books that make up the epic. Clearly it was going to be slow going. At some point, I threw in the towel. But while the concept may have been over-ambitious, the first song was based on a standard I–IV–V blues-style progression, with a pop chorus thrown in and Leonard Cohen–style vocals. I figured it would be a walk in the park.

We were working on "Achilles" when Bilerman arrived with a new crown in his mouth. Soon, four hours had gone by and we still didn't quite have it right. It was gruelling. I wasn't entirely sure why it wasn't working. The song was very much a singer-songwriter sort of thing; perhaps it didn't have room for other instruments. Both Morgan and Bucky kept searching for their parts.

I was perhaps to blame for not focusing enough on what they were doing, as fingerpicking the song and singing its numerous Homeric verses required every ounce of my energy and concentration. Three painful dents surfaced on the fingertips of my left hand. Morgan was coming up with some interesting stuff but was not quite satisfied; he seemed to be suffering through it.

"Maybe we're micromanaging this too much," Bucky said. The trio that had coalesced so well the previous day was now in danger of falling apart.

Bucky needed a cigarette break, so we headed out into the impeccably sunny day. Nobody had matches, and we shot the breeze until finally some guy they knew passed by.

"Do you smoke?" Bucky asked him.

"For a living," the guy said.

We ogled Bilerman's Fiat Spider. The clock was ticking. Today was only meant to be a half day, and at this rate we were going to end up with zilch to show for it.

Back in the control room, Bilerman lent a hand. "Songs are like clothing," he said. "A good song can wear any sort of outfit and still look good. Sometimes it takes getting used to. You might not feel comfortable wearing a tuxedo, but I think it's important to keep an open mind when you first look in the mirror. Because you never know — everyone else who looks at you might think you look great."

Maybe I was having trouble recognizing my song in the new garb.

"Let me ask you," Bilerman said, "what artist comes to mind with your vision of this song? It can be helpful to have a framework."

"I don't know. I never thought of it in that sort of way. It should be spacious, like maybe Lou Reed's 'Walk on the Wild Side' or something by Nick Cave."

"Funny," said Bilerman, "it reminds me of another Nick. Nick Drake."

So the weary band tried again, with slightly more clarity in our heads. We did another, calmer take, and it seemed to work. Better than anything we'd done yet. And it was 3 p.m.; our half day was over.

Morgan, who'd had a rehearsal the previous night *after* our long session, took off on his bike. I felt he might be annoyed with me for some reason; he hadn't made much eye contact. He may well have thought I was getting all micromanagerial on him. But it had been a tough day on the heels of yesterday's long session. Not even a lunch break. For his part, Bucky had a gig that evening with an indie band at Barfly. Session No. 2 thus ended on a worrisome note. After going two-for-two in our first session with "Go Slow" and "Basement Rainbow" in addition to starting "Honey from the Sky," we were now oh-for-two on our most recent attempts.

In the parking lot, Bilerman told me that sometimes with a complicated song a practice session with the band beforehand is a good idea. Or maybe a different bass/drum combination might work better on some songs. His advice to me for the next day: "Start with a simpler song, something more linear." Then he drove off in his black Spider producer-mobile to take his daughter to a piano lesson.

H2T: SESSION NO. 3

IF I WAS APPREHENSIVE before the first session at Hotel2Tango, I was downright worried about our last kick at the can. There was a very good chance that this last day would yield no complete song, which would be a budgetary fiasco and cast heavy doubt on the viability of the project.

I was up at 6 a.m. writing a chord chart for "Sign of Design" and fine-tuning the lyrics for "Cherries." I also replied to an email from Morey. I told him he was welcome to swing by the studio at any point. He was thinking of a visit in the late morning. This made me concerned that the studio team would interpret Morey's visit as a sign of panic, as if he'd been parachuted in from head office to help fix a bad situation. But Morey had been so supportive that I could not disinvite him.

I was at Hotel2Tango before 9 a.m., and Bilerman answered the buzzer, ushering me through the heavy red door.

"Guess what song was in my head last night?" he asked.

"Um, I dunno."

"'Honey from the Sky.'"

In the coffee machine alcove, Bilerman made me an espresso. He showed off a recent acquisition, an LP, "The first record I ever owned," he told me. He'd been thrilled to snag it on eBay. *Fonzie Favorites*.

Bucky and his trusty snare were punctual, even though his Barfly gig had ended at 3 a.m. I asked him how much sleep he had gotten, and the vague answer was not encouraging. Morgan soon breezed in, conspicuously friendly and passing around a fragrant bag of fresh croissants.

We decided to pick up where we left off on "Achilles," which had been so resistant to our efforts. It would have been a shame to abandon the song, as we'd spent so much time on it and made considerable progress. I plugged in my electric guitar to spare my damaged fingertips, but the old maple-bodied Gibson L6 was woefully unable to stay in tune. The neck needed work. Bilerman handed me a sunburst-coloured studio guitar, which coincidentally turned out to be a Gibson L6S, the same obscure model as mine.

While we were playing the song for the zillionth time, with its interminable verses adapted from the blind bard's poem, it occurred to me that maybe I should forget about the closing verse.

"What's that last verse about?" Bilerman wanted to know. "Is it important for the narrative?"

"Well, we can live without it. I've already had to cut a bunch of verses because it was way too long. Homer won't mind." I turned to Morgan and Bucky. "What do you guys think? Another verse, or an instrumental end?" They voted for an instrumental final stretch.

We plugged away at the tune with renewed vigour. Morgan had hit upon some chords that darkly echoed my droning on guitar. Bucky used his kick drum to pound out dramatic punctuation marks. After holding back for the verses, the rhythm section galvanized the choruses. And my idea to remove the regimented click track after the second chorus allowed for a final burst of energy that carried the song to the finish line. Achilles, that stubborn warrior, was finally dispatched.

Next up I'd chosen a "more linear" song, as per Bilerman's suggestion, though I didn't exactly know what he meant by that. Something more even-keeled, without the dramatic ups and downs of "Achilles," was my guess. "Cherries," the calm, steady song about my calm, steady grandfather, seemed like a good candidate.

Morgan hoisted his high-and-mighty upright bass for the occasion. Bucky picked up his brushes (made of metal bristles, providing a softer sound on the snare drum). The song seemed to play itself, the verse flowing into the chorus and back into the verse, minimalist and meditative.

Morey arrived between takes, and I introduced him. He strolled around the recording room, eyeballing what looked to him like a junkyard of vintage equipment. Guitar amps leaned against the walls, effects pedals lined the windowsills, and cables snaked across the wood floor and oriental rugs.

Morey disappeared into the control room, and we had another go at "Cherries." We soon joined Bilerman and Morey for a listen.

"You know what I hear?" Morey said to me.

I knew what he meant by the question—what other instruments he imagined could be layered onto the song.

"What?"

"Tympani."

"Tympani?"

"Yeah, tympani. Triplets. Going *da-ba-boom, da-ba-boom*." He made the percussion instrument, a staple of symphony orchestras, sound perfectly at home in the song.

I asked Bilerman, "Do we have any tympani lying around?"

Morey said that it could be a bass tom drum tuned really low. "Also," he said, "strings."

"Oh yeah? How would we do that? How many string instruments would we need?"

"Oh, it would all be on computer," Morey said.

So we had another song down. And ideas on how to layer it. That made two songs done and dusted before noon. My luck had turned around.

Bilerman was thinking about lunch and passing around a Thai takeout menu. Meanwhile, a man by the name of Garfield, an old-school central European type, had been repairing one of Bilerman's reel-to-reel tape machines. I'd heard the name Garfield mentioned from time to time at the studio. He had some sort of workshop in the basement of the building. On one occasion, Bilerman had gone to get an emergency backup battery from him. Another time, Garfield provided the glue for Morgan's finger.

I invited Morey to stay for lunch, but he had to go. Morgan, meanwhile, was experiencing finger woes again. The beat-up skin on his middle finger kept splitting open. He left at one point to procure some more Krazy Glue.

After Thai noodles in the lunchroom, we got back to work, this time on "Honey from the Sky." After our morning productivity, I no longer feared a debacle. But "Honey" was the song that had sent us into a downward spiral forty hours earlier. Although Morgan was smitten with our most recent version, I remained unconvinced. I suggested that he use his upright bass, knowing that he wouldn't be able to play the catchy riff on that acoustic beast of an instrument.

Bilerman played us a version of "Honey" from two days earlier that had a spirit he liked. We liked it too. It was slower, mellower, restrained. Bilerman's advice: play the song as if our parents were sleeping upstairs and we didn't want to wake them. This was something we could hang our hats on. We went to it. Progress seemed to be in the air, but suddenly:

"Aaarrggh!" Morgan let out a yelp. His finger had cracked open again, and he disappeared to repair it. So as not to lose valuable time, Bilerman suggested that Bucky and I record the tune without Morgan.

Afterwards, we sat in the control room, peering through the glass at Morgan, who — Krazy Glued back together again — slow danced with his standup bass and laid down gorgeous lines over the drums and guitar.

With song number three behind us, I could relax a bit and appreciate the surroundings. Late-afternoon sunshine filtered through the frosted-glass bricks, casting a soft glow on the burnished wood instruments and muted tones of peach, orange, and burgundy that coloured the room. Bilerman's venerable dog, Gus, was wandering about.

At one point, Bucky pulled a prank on Morgan by sending him a sophomoric text. Some comic antics followed.

The atmosphere was suddenly slap-happy.

"You never warned me that they're like this," I told Bilerman.

"First time I've seen them like this," he said.

We had time for one more song. I asked the rhythm section whether they preferred to do a country-inflected song or an R&B-type number, and I played them snippets of each tune on my iPhone. Morgan said the R&B song would require more planning and suggested we try the countrified item, "Perfect Shell."

This was the song meant to feature Rebecca Campbell, who'd sung it so stunningly when we jammed in Toronto. To suit her vocal range, I'd transposed the key from D to A with the result that it was out—way out—of my own range. I couldn't sing it. Morgan and Bucky, though, said they needed to hear some vocals to make sense of the song. So as we ran through it, I sang in a half-hearted falsetto. Several takes later, they started speaking to me in a mocking falsetto. I retaliated by singing the next take in a very low-speaking croak. It sounded a bit like Lou Reed. Weirdly, it didn't sound all that bad. My colleagues, Bilerman in particular, insisted that I'd stumbled on a nifty vocal idea worth keeping.

Again and again we played the song. Bucky threw in variations when he counted us in, such as "One and a two and you know what to do." After repeated run-throughs with zero time between takes, I told them I could use a few seconds to catch my breath. Singing the song again and again with barely a second's rest was an aerobic exercise. Plus I was trying to put some feeling into the effort.

"There's a lot of emotional investment in these songs," I said.

They chortled. "Take all the time you need."

A few seconds later, we were into another take, this time getting it down, making it seem easy. Thirty minutes remained on the studio clock. Rather than fritter the time away, we recorded Morey's tympani idea. Bilerman set Bucky up with a tuned-down bass tom, and he went into a closed room to record the percussion. He then recorded some "egg" (a shaker sound), also over the chorus, and that was the last track of the adventure, an adventure that narrowly avoided becoming a misadventure. Four songs in one day. That brought our grand total to six. Which felt respectable.

Morgan and Bucky packed up their gear and got ready to skedaddle. "I don't think you realize how good your songs are," Morgan told me as we bid each other goodbye. Shucks. I was paying him for this, but he wouldn't stretch the truth, would he? He also said that when the time came to do the final vocal tracks, I should try singing them myself.

"I thought you might have been a bit annoyed with me yesterday, for some reason," I said. "But today everything seemed fine and you were warm and cuddly."

"So you're saying," he replied, "that I'm a moody son of a bitch?"

I hugged Morgan and Bucky goodbye. It seemed like a long time ago that they'd greeted each other with hugs and I'd felt like a distant outsider. By now a certain camaraderie had been forged in the six-song crucible at Hotel2Tango.

Morgan's girlfriend, Lisa, just back from a tour, arrived to pick him up. Bucky, snare in hand, raced off, anxious to catch the hockey game which, unless the Canadiens were to win, would be the last opportunity to see his team for five months.

I helped Morgan carry his gear into his car and then returned to the lunchroom, where Bilerman was munching on a croissant left over from Morgan's morning stash. I joined him, musing about the session. "I guess we did okay in the end," I said.

"Six songs in three sessions is actually very good," he said, "considering Bucky and Morgan had to learn the material as well as perform it. Bands who know their material inside-out come in and still take two or three hours on a song."

At home I watched the Canadiens lose again. Destroyed 6–1. But I celebrated a personal victory of sorts. Three sessions in a big studio with pro musicians was a lifelong dream. I felt as if I'd accomplished something I'd been waiting to do for years and years—in fact, for most of my life. The fingers on my left hand were shot and sore, heavily callused and deeply creased by phosphor bronze strings. But all I felt was soulful uplift.

CAPTURING REALITY

"**I** NEVER WANTED TO be a rock star," Morey was telling me.

We were having a coffee at one of our haunts. Morey was describing how when he started out as a musician, his dream was to be a studio guitarist, what he called a "chameleon guitar player."

"I wanted to bring songs to life, whether the music was heavy metal or country," he said. "I wanted to do what's right for the music to make it work as music."

Turning the conversation to my project, Morey suggested I had to decide what I wanted to do now that the "bed tracks" (bass, drums, rhythm guitar, and vocals) had been recorded at H2T.

"You could spend the rest of your life going in circles on this and spending a lot of money," he said. "Now that you've reached the stage of bed tracks, where do you want to be in the process?"

From his point of view there were three types of people in my situation:

1. The person who knows what he wants and how to get there.
2. The person who knows what he wants when he hears it. It can take a long time.
3. The person who doesn't know what he wants, so needs a producer and/or outside musicians. A third party becomes the driving force.

Morey was of the opinion that I was person number two.

"This past stage was hard," Morey said. "The next stage will be hard."

"When does it get easy?"

"It doesn't."

I asked Morey, not for the first time, if he'd take one of my songs and record it in his "lab." Maybe get his daughter to sing. He said he'd give it a try, though he'd agreed to do such things in the past (such as reworking "Grace of Love") but had yet to deliver.

He liked the creative freedom of doing it in his lab — "everything in my box" — as opposed to, say, in Hotel2Tango. But he warned me that my music would likely turn out very different in his box. "I'd treat one of your songs as a song. You might be shocked by the result." It would be very different than my approach, which — unavoidably, he said — centred around me as the artist. "You're one guy with one instrument, and you can only present the songs one way. Even in the studio" — Hotel2Tango, with Morgan and Bucky and Bilerman — "they're running with your voice . . .

with you as a singer-songwriter. They don't have a lot of time, so the style tends to get pigeonholed."

We drained our cappuccinos. "So," I asked him, "what did you think of Hotel2Tango as a studio?"

"I expected something more sophisticated," he said. "It was like being in someone's parents' basement who collected stuff." The vintage equipment and instruments lying around was "prehistoric stuff" that he remembered from a quarter century ago—cables zig-zagging around the place, weird old keyboards. He didn't mention Gus the dog.

"It's a spit-and-Kleenex-type studio," Morey said.

"Really?"

"Not to say you don't get good results there."

I asked Morey how he thought Hotel2Tango compared with Eli Krantzberg's basement setup.

Again his reply surprised me. "Eli has done the most you can do in a basement. Eli's sound is cleaner, tighter, and more transparent. Eli tries to capture the sound in its most natural state. He's a master manipulator... a technician. He makes it as pure as possible and adds effects later."

"And Bilerman?"

Bilerman's approach at Hotel2Tango was the opposite, according to Morey. Bilerman captured the sound "as is. There could be a buzzing sound from a three-guitar stand or something rattling on the ceiling. Or there's an amp in the corner with loose knobs that are shaking. That's his vibe," said Morey. "Bilerman's thing is playing the song a million times and capturing the magic of that one moment."

The difference between Bilerman and Morey reflects a long-standing aesthetic divide when it comes to sound recording. Starting with Thomas Edison, there have been two philosophies about high fidelity: to capture sound as it truly exists, as if the listener were right there in the same room as the musicians, or to shape sound with no loyalty to the reality of performance.

The early, acoustic recordings tried to reflect that "authentic" aesthetic. Electrical recordings, which came later and used microphones and amplification, were criticized by purists like Edison for modifying reality. The debate foreshadowed the analogue-versus-digital dispute.

When magnetic tape arrived on the scene, editing became possible, thus further allowing performances to be altered through the slicing and dicing of tape. Then came multi-track recording, in which the musicians no longer had to play at the same time and eventually sixty-four separate tracks could be layered piecemeal into a song; that strayed far from the idea of capturing reality.

Finally, computer-based recording, which enables all manner of digital alteration and processing, has allowed a disconnection from the actual playing of real instruments. In his fascinating history of sound recording, Greg Milner wonders why anyone but audiophiles might find it desirable for recordings to mirror real life. He notes that for genres like techno and hip-hop, there never was a real-time event that the music is based on. As for your "average radio pop song," it "may have the structure of a self-contained performance," writes Milner, "...but there is a good chance that none of these musicians were ever in the same room at the same time—if the record contains samples, the musicians may be separated by decades—so what event, exactly, is the recording?"

The authenticity factor behind recordings is almost

always a matter of degree. At one end of the spectrum is simply capturing a live band's performance — bottling the magic the way Bilerman likes to do. At the other end is music created track by track, overdubbing one instrument at a time, possibly over a long period of time, and sometimes in more than one studio.

What recording route musicians take has to do with personal taste, as well as the budget, genre of music, time constraints, size of the band, and need for space. For example, you can't capture the live performance of drums, standup bass, guitar, and vocals, much less more instruments, if you're recording in a space as small as Krantzberg's studio.

Other sonic issues, such as digital manipulation versus analogue "reality," have to do with personal taste — and, apparently, demographics. When I was at Hotel2Tango, several copies of a sound engineering magazine called *Tape Op* were lying around the control room. I took a bunch home, and though I had to wade through much gearhead verbiage, some of the articles helped place my studio experience in a greater context.

"The tones people enjoy are changing generationally," said Jesse Cannon, a producer who has recorded Animal Collective and worked with the Cure and Limp Bizkit. "If you were eight to twelve years old in 1998, one of your first musical experiences was the dawn of the age of Auto-Tune — that's the year Cher's 'Believe' was released," he told the *Tape Op* interviewer. "All through your formative years you heard a lot of Auto-Tune and early Pro Tools recordings." As a result, "A lot of the younger musicians of today have a sound that is super digital. I never thought ten years ago I'd have people say to me, 'That sounds WAY too warm.'

They don't want harmonics; just cold and clinical. On the other hand, if I don't distort things to hell with my older clients they think it sounds lifeless. There's a huge generation gap brewing when it comes to harmonics."

At Hotel2Tango, I'd thrown my lot in with the hubbub of live performance, of capturing reality. This was Bilerman's preferred modus operandi. But he wasn't dogmatic about live recording. In my case, the "live" aspect would be far from absolute. The bed tracks were live. Yet I'd be returning to the studio in many cases to replace guitar and vocal guide tracks with more polished performances. Plus I'd eventually be adding guitar solos and new instruments. Still, the kernel of those recordings contained the spark and energy, as well as the frailties and imperfections, of live performance.

During one break in the sessions, I had asked Bilerman to elaborate on his recording approach. He had much to say in favour of live performances. Before the advent of multi-track recording, he told me, "The stakes [in the studio] were higher. It was more of a performance; artists would approach recording in the studio the same way as playing a show, where there was no net and you'd have to commit. To me that makes recorded music better."

He continued, "That's not to say that, once they introduced multi-track recording and the ability to overdub and/or fix things, music got worse. I think there's an infinite number of records made that way, the *creating* way, as opposed to the *documentation* way. We'll call it the *creating* way, whereby you crack an egg and then you add some sugar and then you add some flour and you stir it all together. There's been some incredible records made that way, but there's also been some records made that way that have been really antiseptic and devoid of life and just so far removed from people playing music together in a room. Those records don't inspire me."

A FEW DAYS after my Hotel2Tango sessions, Bilerman emailed me temp mixes of the six songs. They definitely sounded more warm and energetic than coolly antiseptic. But it took time for me to get my head around the live performances of a band that had been thrown together on the spot.

"Go Slow" and "Cherries" sounded speedy; "Perfect Shell" was lacklustre; and neither of the two very different versions of "Honey from the Sky" were what I'd originally had in mind. "Achilles" was hard to listen to because I was sloppily playing an unfamiliar studio guitar in what was meant to be a temporary guide track, and the song became a wild bucking bronco after the bridge. Other details seemed problematic. I wasn't sure about a Latin-style vamp on "Cherries" after every chorus. And though I'd wanted raucous drum fills in the interlude for "Go Slow," the results were sounding bombastic.

Disaster.

Or was it? Maybe some elements could be fixed. Maybe I was too close to judge. But the feeling was not a good one. As the days progressed, I went through Kübler-Ross's stages of grief, from denial to anger to bargaining to depression.

Then, happily, acceptance kicked in.

At one point, I started to really like the songs, even my voice. It felt as if I were in a band, warts and all. I was singing my songs, and Bucky and Morgan were expertly backing me with verve and beauty, captured honestly and free of artifice in a bona fide live performance.

BATTLEFIELD MIND

BACK IN THE 1990S, I used to frequent a particular dive bar on as many Sunday nights as I could. The attraction was Michael Jerome Browne (MJB), the most compelling blues artist, bar none, I had ever seen. I have a lot of time for blues icons like Robert Johnson and B. B. King. The pre-electric Delta blues style, rubbing shoulders with country and folk, is right up my aesthetic alley. As a guitar player, I have the blues DNA in my bloodstream. But I'm not the most devout of blues fans. Most contemporary purveyors of the genre leave me cold. Caged in the iron bars of I–IV–V progressions, the predictability can grow monotonous. And the definition of art that grabs you may well be that which straddles the line of predictability/unpredictability, novel/familiar, safe/risky. The precise ratio varies from cerebral cortex to cerebral cortex.

In the dimly lit, thinly attended G Sharp Bar on St. Laurent Boulevard, MJB was never overly predictable or safe, to my ear. His blues ranged far and wide, encompassing soul, gospel, Tin Pan Alley, slide, Cajun, ballads, and all manner of backwoodsy material. His guitar playing was superb, his choice of material intriguing, and his voice manna from the harmonic spheres.

It had a stamp of authenticity that seemed to have been pressed somewhere south of these here parts half a century ago. And there was a legend at street level, the story being that he wheeled into town from Chicago when he was a kid, already a blues encyclopedia who knew everything and could play anything. He supposedly joined the Stephen Barry Blues Band, local veterans of the art form, at some precocious age, like thirteen. That was the story.

I had thought about MJB vis à vis one of my songs, "Battlefield Mind," a crudely simple composition meant for a high, lonesome voice that might belong to him. When I picked up my guitar after my Bach phase, out came this primitive expectoration, a raw thing that purged all the high-minded music that was so far above my head in terms of technical playability.

I googled MJB and was delighted to see just how many awards and critical hosannas he'd accumulated in the categories of blues artist, acoustic artist, singer, and guitarist. During those G Sharp days, I used to think it a shame that there were so few people in the audience to appreciate the performances. Happily, his talent had won out in the end.

Mustering some cyber-courage, I emailed him cold, introducing myself and explaining that I was trying to get various singers to sing original songs that I was recording. I had one or two in mind for him. Might he conceivably be interested?

MJB emailed me back and said that he remembered me because his early press kit featured some praise I'd written in the Montreal *Gazette* when I was its pop music critic. Send along the tunes, he suggested. Which I nervously did. I emailed the version of "Battlefield Mind" sung by Rebecca Campbell in Toronto at her kitchen table (I had since earmarked another song for her), then "Achilles" and "Another Man's Crime." I wanted to maximize my chances by giving him a choice.

To my immense pleasure, much back-and-forth email-ing ensued, though at a snail's pace, since MJB seemed to forever be on tour. He first asked for lyrics to the songs, a good sign. Then he wanted to know what they were about. Then he requested the sheet music.

His emails contained a curiously double-barrelled name at the sender line: B. A. Markus & Michael Jerome Browne. I wondered who B. A. Markus might be and assumed he was probably a manager or agent privy to all of Browne's artistic dealings. Still, it seemed odd, as if someone was eavesdrop-ping on our correspondence. Or, for all I knew, ghostwriting MJB's end of things.

Around this time, I was teaching a writing workshop at the Atwater Library. One evening before class, a bespec-tacled woman stood nearby while I was chatting with some workshop participants. When the conversation ebbed, she approached me.

"Hi, I'm B. A. Markus," she said, handing me a CD. "Michael Browne wanted you to have this."

It was a copy of his most recent recording, *The Road Is Dark*.

Surprised, I thanked her for the disc and asked what her connection to MJB was.

"I'm his partner," she said.

"Business partner or personal partner?"

"Both."

They lived together, had a couple of young kids, and B. A. (Bee, as her friends call her) also wrote many of the lyrics for his original songs. She was a blogger as well and was coincidentally enrolled in the writing workshop that took place just before mine.

I wondered whether the CD she'd given me was a sort of consolation prize, meaning that MJB wasn't interested in my tone-deaf tunes but was being very civil about it all. Yet, not too many days later, another email appeared from B. A. and MJB. The verdict had finally rolled in.

"The only song of the three that I might be able to do is 'Battlefield Mind,'" he wrote.

And so began our collaboration. The blues master soon emailed to ask whether I was okay with rewriting some of the lyrics so that the number of syllables would better conform to his phrasing. That's the way he worked with Bee, he said. We could meet up and discuss the words, "kind of like when actors workshop a play."

I met MJB not at one of the many artsy cafés near where he lives in Mile End, but at a no-frills bakery, fittingly called Maestro, on St-Urbain. We grabbed croissants and coffee and occupied one of the very few tables in the joint. There was a slightly surreal quality to the fact that a musician I'd all but worshipped so long ago was about to channel his talent into one of my songs.

MJB wore a purple jacket over a grey sweatshirt. A pair of hot-pink reading glasses were perched at the edge of his nose. His greying hair was in the genre of bouffant. I wondered whether Tommy the barber, whose vintage shop was nearby and who used to cut my hair with idiosyncratic flair, was responsible for his do.

MJB unfolded a printed copy of my lyrics for "Battlefield Mind" and pulled a pencil with a bobble-head eraser from behind his ear. I felt a bit self-conscious having the song's opaque lyrics placed under his microscope.

We went over them line by line. MJB had counted the syllables (or, in musical terms, "beats") for every line and wanted them to be more consistent. I'd gotten around the differentiation by elongating some words when I sang the tune. But he was more rigorous. Some lines were fine; others were missing beats.

"The scanning of that line is good," he said of the third line of the chorus. "But the word *anyway* is weak." Content did not escape his bobble-headed pencil. What did he mean by *scanning*? MJB explained that good scanning means the right words are stressed and that the song "sings well."

I told him I was happy to rewrite the words to suit his singing. The changes he wanted would not alter the music, just the words, and I knew I could improve them while making the syllables to measure.

Over the next little while, I tinkered with the lyrics. My desire to satisfy MJB made it a time-consuming process. A line like the second one, *in a land of plenty*, which had felt perfectly timed for my phrasing, was now missing two syllables. They were not so easy to find.

In a car-ni-val of plenty? Not quite the imagery I had in mind for the song. I eventually settled on *a broken land of plenty*.

In the chorus—*anyway it's a dangerous time / when the battlefield is on your mind*—I axed the *anyway* (he was right; it was weak) and replaced it with *imaginary enemy lines / when the battlefield is on your mind.*

I emailed my revisions, he made suggestions, I revised the revisions, all while MJB toured in places where wifi was hard to come by. At one point I sent him a phone recording in which I sang the new lines. We hammered out an agreement.

MJB next requested that he select the drummer and bassist who would accompany him on the song. He wanted to play alongside his stalwart rhythm section, the legendary Stephen Barry on bass and John McColgan on drums. I was more than fine with that. But at the same time something uncomfortable dawned on me. I would not be playing on the tune. My musical services were not required.

I suppose this should have been obvious to me. MJB was a black belt of the blues, to the nth degree. How could I possibly fit in, unless it was to shoehorn my ego into the mix?

Soon the point became moot. He emailed me a down-and-dirty iPad recording of "Battlefield Mind." It was spellbinding. So spellbinding that I wondered whether a studio version was necessary. His rhythm guitar, slide work, and high, lonesome vocals handled everything that needed handling.

It sounded like an artifact from the 1930s Mississippi Delta. As if an old recording by some Blind Orange Jackson had been unearthed. (An amusing adage states that you can convincingly come up with the name of an old-time blues icon by combining a handicap, a fruit, and the name of an ex-president.) It was brilliant. And to even consider having the composer play some guitar, even if it were to be buried in the final mix, was silly.

I had booked a session at Hotel2Tango to record the tune. The day before that date, there was a rehearsal at Browne's home. By the time I arrived, the bassist and drummer, as well as B. A. Markus, were chatting in a cozy room off the kitchen. A piano leaned against one wall, a guitar hung from another, and the artwork of children was everywhere to be seen.

I told Stephen Barry that I'd been a big fan since I was a kid who wore out the grooves of his *Stephen Barry Band Live* album, a classic in my memory bank, recorded at the Hôtel Iroquois in Old Montreal.

"Oh, you silver-tongued flatterer," Barry said.

He was looking nearly as venerable as his upright bass, which was made in 1939 — a very good year, he later told me, for that make of bass. As a bass player he was of a very good vintage himself, the leader of the city's most enduring blues band for more than five decades.

I have heard the Stephen Barry Band play all over town, in parks, at festivals, in clubs. I even jammed with them at an open mic night they used to host at a bar called La Bohème on St. Laurent Boulevard.

After some banter, the musicians took up position, Barry hoisting his beast of four strings and drummer John McColgan, shiny pate, bespectacled, employing only a snare drum and brushes. MJB was seated with a scholarly air, guitar in hand, brass slide on his pinky finger, a page of lyrics copied out in fat Magic Marker on a music stand.

There was some discussion about the drum beat and the bassline for the chorus, but it proceeded basically as MJB had played it on his field recording. I offered a few suggestions here and there. It was straightforward. I sang on a few go-throughs so that MJB could concentrate on his guitar playing. But he'd transposed the key to suit his voice and the song was now in F-sharp, not A, with the result that I couldn't sing it in either a high or a low register. My voice was way off, but it filled in the blanks somewhat. Two hours had suddenly come and gone, and "the boys," as MJB referred to them, had to go.

The next day, we met at Hotel2Tango. Stephen Barry had never been there before, but he told me that he'd dreamed of the place, and dreamed about it in great detail. It apparently conformed to his reveries.

Bilerman seemed pleased that I'd brought what he called my "A-Team" to the studio. He made espressos for the trio and soon was discussing drums with McColgan and setting up mics for what was to be a live recording. MJB would record his voice and guitar solo separately, but bass/drums/ rhythm guitar would be captured live off the floor.

They were positioned in the room exactly as Bucky, Morgan, and myself had been months earlier. I was in a little room off the control room, where I would be "singing" the song as a guide for the musicians. The timing of how MJB came out of the chorus and into the verse was tricky, and I worried that I'd screw up what might otherwise be magical takes. But I focused as best I could, shouting "Solo!" when it came to the guitar solo that would not be recorded until later. We had a very good version in no time at all.

The trio kerplunked on the couch in the control room and listened to the recording. MJB then sang the vocal track and cast it in stone on his very first attempt. For insurance he did two more versions, just in case we wanted to cut and paste some small imperfections. But his voice was so authentic and the performance so organic that I knew I wouldn't want to alter so much as a letter.

There was some light-hearted discussion about whether MJB's vocals could be Auto-Tuned. "Auto-Tune doesn't make sense for the blues," MJB said, because the blues revolves around some notes that are intentionally flattened, which makes them "blue."

"With a twist of the knob," said Stephen Barry, "you can eliminate the blues!"

As a joke, Bilerman Auto-Tuned one verse of vocals from the song we were working on. The pitch correction sounded nonsensical, the blue screen no match for the actual blues.

"Of the six records I've made, only one note has ever been Auto-Tuned," MJB said. He added that it was unavoidable, to fix a mistake played by another musician during a live recording.

Back to "Battlefield Mind" — all that remained was a guitar solo. MJB went back into the tracking room and, using a large brass slide on his pinky finger, recorded a few versions, digging up precious material from his 1935 National Trojan resonator guitar. I asked him if he could add some more licks towards the end of the song. He obliged with alchemy, and the session was over.

I walked "the boys" to the door, thanking them profusely and hearing a bit more about Stephen Barry's dream of Hotel2Tango. "Isn't there supposed to be a vending machine downstairs somewhere?" he asked.

"There is, in the basement of the studio," I said. "Was that in your dream as well?"

"No, I think I knew that."

MJB left soon afterwards. I was touched by all the work

he'd put into the song. He was no mercenary. If he does a song he does a song, and it bears his fingerprints and stamp of approval. I was honoured.

I'd see MJB at a later date, when Bilerman would mix the song. He wanted to be there.

Meanwhile, Bilerman had developed a nasty headache that doses of Tylenol, coffee, and chocolate had not quelled. I felt responsible; the song was called "Battlefield Mind."

UNDERBELLY

THE WEATHER HAD BEEN steamy and rainy, but I was very glad not to have to layer my body like a pop song. I walked over to the Jonah James Café in shorts and sandals to meet Morey for one of our regular tête-à-têtes. He had a lot to say about the rapidly changing business of making music.

There is a subculture, a new reality driven by young people, that Morey calls the "underbelly" of the industry. "Not one of Hayley's friends buys music," he said. "What they do is go on to YouTube with a computer program that downloads audio from the site and installs the music in their iTunes software. Free as the breeze. You can forget about making money, or at least a lot of money, with a recording."

"That's what I hear," I said, sipping a macchiato.

"The recording of a song is now a business card," he continued. Hayley's business cards were circulating on the Internet. With her captivating voice set to Morey's lush productions on YouTube, she was starting to create embry-onic buzz in the "underbelly."

A case in point: Morey and Hayley recorded a version of Lana Del Rey's cover of the Nirvana tune "Heart-Shaped Box." Lana Del Rey is a former Fordham University student of metaphysics and a self-described "gangsta-style Nancy Sinatra." Two years earlier, a video Del Rey made for her debut single, "Video Games," had gone viral on YouTube, to the tune of twenty million views.

But her cover of "Heart-Shaped Box" existed only in a live recording. There was no studio version by Del Rey when Morey and Hayley uploaded their cover on YouTube. It created much interest there and on Tumblr.

"Hundreds of thousands of posts," Morey said. "It went crazy."

It went crazy based on total misinformation. The thou-sands of young listeners who were posting and linking Hay-ley's audio clip were under the impression that it was in fact Lana Del Rey, not Hayley Richman. All the buzz centred on the mistaken belief that it was an actual studio recording made by Del Rey.

Morey had no love lost for the old business model for musicians. He remembered how high the odds were stacked against making it. He never saw a record deal that gave the artist back more than five dollars' gross per record. That in and of itself would be fine, but there was something called a "charge back" in which the artists owed the record com-pany a huge amount of money based on umpteen expenses. Those expenses might include three months in the studio— $75,000 to $100,000, for a small-budget record—plus more for promotion, another $20,000 for a video, and then room and board and spending money while the band was touring to drive sales of the album. "Think of all the records you'd have to sell to recoup that," he said.

When Morey was gigging for a living, he'd have had to sell something in the neighbourhood of two hundred thousand records just to break even. Now he could make a record—or a dozen records—for the three or four grand all his gear and software cost. And if Hayley actually got to the next level, like any artist today that breaks out on their own, she would get a far better deal with a record company, as they would not have sunk any money into her.

So for bands that don't make it in a huge way, selling fifty thousand records can earn them decent money, because they get to keep virtually all the income from the sale. Bands today also have social media at their fingertips to promote their work, and iTunes and other digital distributors to sell it (to the extent that consumers are buying and not pirating or streaming music for a pittance on online music services like Spotify).

"The way it worked before," Morey told me, "fifty thousand in sales would have meant the record company dumping you."

One of the rock bands Morey played in made a cassette of songs that cost them eight dollars and sold for ten dollars. As a revenue model, this left something to be desired. The distribution method—selling them at live shows—was also limited.

"Now you can sit in your underwear in your basement and sell your stuff all over the world," Morey said. "And if you want a string section, you got it. Nor do you have to worry about the bass player not showing up because he's hungover...But you're no longer a rock star. You're more like a minstrel. Personally I like the idea."

To sum up the changes in the industry: there is no longer a traditional gatekeeper. In his *Tape Op* interview, Jesse Cannon gave a very good description of this new landscape. If you were a musician fifteen years ago *not* making mainstream pop songs, he said, "you had to hope to find some kind of gatekeeper—a label, manager, or booking agent with enough connections and time to try to push you out to the world. You'd need to spend thousands of dollars, press CDs, and get them to stores. Now if you have a unique vision, fans can choose to elevate you for a minimum investment.

"Music," Cannon said, "has been democratized. Thousands of bloggers curate to small, specific audiences and spread the word. It's easier than ever...There is an amazing flattening of the music world happening."

That's the new musical world Morey had been telling me about, the world that his daughter was thriving in. Hayley had in fact just been named YouTube Artist of the Month by an online magazine called *StarCentral*.

"She did nothing to get it," Morey said. "Is it going to generate anything? Who knows? But there's a huge underbelly of activity. It's a subculture. You've got to sniff it out. You've got to find it. Shaharah, Jo—these people may believe in the old model, but it's dead. Maybe they should embrace the new order."

YouTube is certainly the new order—the new way of listening to music, the new radio, the new MTV, even the new way for record labels to discover talent. "It has supplanted radio as the main way American teenagers listen to new music," the *New York Times* had reported a week earlier, citing a Nielsen survey. A few months before that, the Billboard Hot 100, that venerable singles chart, had announced that it was incorporating YouTube plays into its formula for calculating hit songs.

We rose from the table at Jonah James, and Morey said, "I have some news for you."

"You do?"

"I've started working on one of your songs."

BACK TO THE BASEMENT

THE NUCLEI OF SEVEN songs were stored in the computer at Hotel2Tango. Add that to the four songs I was happy about in Krantzberg's studio, and I had the makings of an album. I got in touch with Krantzberg and made plans to finish those four tunes.

He asked me to walk around the side of his house and go through the back door, which I did, noticing Mariam's colourful lingerie drying on the clothesline. They were now man and wife. The wedding, at McGill University's Faculty Club, reportedly went well, as did the honeymoon, spent at the Château Montebello resort in western Quebec, touted as the largest log cabin in North America.

I hadn't seen Krantzberg for a long while; it felt like I'd returned to my childhood home. I was there to lay down electric guitar tracks for "Sign of Design" and "Firewall" — the song formerly known as "Unstoppable." (It had not lasted very long as the re-named "Inflammable," after Shaharah took one look at the revised lyrics and said the new title did not roll off the tongue very well. Rewritten yet again, it became "Firewall.")

In the basement studio, I recorded some rhythm guitar and also injected funk-style riffs for interludes into each song. In one case, I used a wah-wah pedal that Nathalie had given me once upon a time, on a sweet impulse purchase.

Everything went swimmingly and I was pleased with the results. Krantzberg even gave me a professional counting tip for when I had four measures to keep track of: "The first digit of the 1-2-3-4 refers to the measure you're on, like this: 1-2-3-4, 2-2-3-4, 3-2-3-4, 4-2-3-4 . . ."

We took a break so I could eat the cheese sandwich I had packed for lunch, and sat outside on the deck, bras and panties flying overhead. Mariam joined us and we talked about the wedding. She'd worn her mother's dress for the ceremony and switched to a pink designer-label item for the party. Krantzberg had worn a navy suit with a pink pocket square, a hundred-dollar shirt, and a striped tie with pink in it. He joked about how much he'd had to learn about clothing, quizzing me on rarefied fashion terminology.

"Do you know what Louis heels are?"

"Um, can't say that I do."

"A boat-neck dress?"

"No idea."

A Unitarian celebrant performed the mixed Jewish-Muslim ceremony. Poems by Atwood, Auden, and e e Cummings were recited by friends.

There were two bands: a trio including an accordion that played old-time classics, and a jazz quartet. Songs from the bride's and groom's favourite movies were featured. A cousin from Ottawa, who still worked in the family shoe business, showed up in pink shoes designed to look like animal feet.

Later, as I was packing up, Krantzberg said, "You know, people are always asking if it feels different to be married. And you know what? The answer is yes! The reason seems to be that I'm no longer available and women know that. Feels different after the single life."

IT HAD BEEN more than six months since I'd first approached Shaharah at the pub. "Another Man's Crime" had been the icebreaker. The jury was still out on that song. But her singing was getting along with two other songs like a house on fire.

"Firewall" was tailor-made for the R&B singer. And "Sign of Design," which I transposed to suit the key she was most comfortable singing in, also felt made to measure.

Both songs had some soulful DNA. "Firewall" even had some James Brown thermodynamics, given the funky ninth chord that governs the song. Few chords, if any, bring to mind a particular style of music as convincingly as a ninth chord. Strum an open G chord on an acoustic guitar and it will arguably sound like the start of a country song. But strike a D9 chord twice — a downwards strum followed quickly by an upwards hit — and you're suddenly on a dance floor with the godfather of soul.

As things stood, the recordings of "Firewall" and "Sign of Design" consisted only of my guitar playing, Shaharah's lead vocals, and a click track that was keeping our rhythm steady. It was time to flesh things out in the studio. And

it occurred to me that maybe I could get Shaharah's bassist and drummer to play on the songs. Her singing was
so powerfully R&B that I thought it would benefit from a
similarly soulful rhythm section. I'd been super impressed
with her band, Soulvation, and it seemed logical that her
regular bassist and drummer would blend well on these
two songs. Shaharah asked them whether they'd do it for a
fee, and they agreed.

The session took place on one of the hottest days of what
had been an insufferably hot summer. I was the first to arrive
at Studio K., and the bass player, Greg Provo, turned up
not long afterwards. He had dreads, a knit grey cap, a blue
T-shirt, a gold necklace, and the name of his girlfriend tat-
tooed on his right arm. Like most everyone else in the city
on such a sweltering day, he was wearing sandals. Krantzberg, in a T-shirt that plugged the magazine ELECTRONIC
MUSICIAN on the front and declared that he was SERIOUSLY
OBSESSED on the back, set the bassist up on a chair. I gave
Provo the chord charts for the first song.

The drummer, Paul Lizzi, was late. I called him on his
cell, and he said he was down the street getting something
to drink and would be there soon. In the meantime, I started
working with Provo on his bassline for "Firewall." It didn't
require much work on my part, as his initial attempts were
pretty fabulous. He had the feel. It was interesting to me
how his mere placement of the notes — not necessarily many
notes or super-complex clusters of them — gave the song
the groove I'd hoped for. The timing of his note placement
might be just ahead or behind the beat, mere fractions in
time, but that fraction made all the difference.

Lizzi, the drummer, finally showed up. "Sorry I'm late,"

he said. A man of about thirty, he had a mohawk haircut and a blue tank top emblazoned with CAPTAIN AMERICA. Quickly getting behind Krantzberg's drum kit, he wanted to hear the first song.

Whereas Provo was laid back and laconic, Lizzi was a juggernaut. At the signoff of Lizzi's email, where you often find corporate credentials, the drummer described himself as: " * Boundary Bustin' Artist * YouTube Star * Mashup King * Diesel Sponsored * Probably on Stage * "

"Paul Lizzi is not your typical artist," goes the promotional blurb on his YouTube channel. "Beyond infectious beats, the Montreal-based musician has added his own vocals and cool personal style to his act."

A few years earlier, Lizzi had released his first single, "Drum Luvin'," which boasted a *Mad Max*–style action video in which Lizzi played drums in the back of a pickup truck and interacted with "sexy captives" and "sexy aliens." He twirled his sticks, brandished a futuristic gun in a desert wasteland, and rhymed "chillin'" with "Bob Dylan." His YouTube channel also promoted the drummer as a fashion model.

In Krantzberg's basement, Lizzi and Provo began playing the song with headphones on, and two things were immediately clear to me: Lizzi is not a background sort of musician; and secondly, he lives up to his own hype. As Krantzberg played back the guitars and vocals previously recorded for "Firewall," Lizzi was smashing the hell out of the cymbals and unleashing a litany of fills. It sounded splendiferous, well on its way to being a finished product. But Lizzi expressed dissatisfaction.

"The guitar is putting me in a box," he said.

That was my guitar playing, two tracks of it. I fessed up and wanted to know what the problem was.

"It's the same kind of box I'm in when we do that James Brown song," he said to Provo.

Now that was the sort of box I could live in. "Yeah, those ninth chords on guitar really scream James Brown," I said. "But I don't mind being boxed in like that."

"The guitar is going off. I'd rather play without it," said Lizzi.

Provo agreed that the guitar — which he pronounced *gi*-tar — was indeed slightly off, timing-wise, here and there. I suggested that Krantzberg remove the wah-wah electric guitar track, which was rhythmically loose. And so they ran through it again, listening to my one remaining guitar part and the gorgeous vocals of Shaharah.

It still wasn't quite jelling. By now I had a bit of experience with session musicians and was getting better at directing traffic.

"You guys are doing great stuff," I told Lizzi and Provo — they were. "We're nearly where we want to be. But think of the song as having four different parts. The tune is essentially one groove. The differences between the verse and the chorus and the bridge are minimal. So our challenge is to give each of the sections their own personality."

We ran through it again, improving every step of the way, yet Provo somehow didn't sound as great playing alongside Lizzi as he had before the drummer arrived. The two weren't "locking" as bass and drums aspire to do. I suggested Provo record his part alone. They were amenable, and a super-smooth bassline was recorded right away. Then Lizzi added the drum part, requesting that my guitar be completely removed. I was cueing him through the various sections, and Provo sometimes signalled time with a pumped fist. For the interlude I asked Lizzi to try something sparse on the floor tom before exploding back into the solo break, which he did with superlative results.

Krantzberg wondered whether we wanted to take a break and get some sunshine — the mercury was skyrocketing. Provo said he preferred to keep working through until we finished the job so he could get outside and enjoy the weather. We kept at it, moving to "Sign of Design," with its straightforward construction.

Mariam soon appeared with a tray of water bottles. "I just think you should know that there's a somewhat pungent atmosphere in here," she said in a decorous manner that would not have been out of place in the American South.

The four males cooped up inside the small space on a sweltering day returned to the job at hand. We finished "Sign of Design" fairly quickly.

Afterwards, Krantzberg and I took a little walk in the blast-furnace afternoon. The whole session had lasted less than four hours, and I felt the results were spectacular. Provo and Lizzi were super players, and these songs were in their sphere (aside from the *gi*-tar being a little off). Krantzberg had been very diplomatic; as an expert drummer he probably could have said many things while the session was in progress, but he limited his interventions to a couple of technical points.

"My drums never before sounded the way they sounded with him playing," Krantzberg told me.

"Why is that?"

"He was playing the cymbals really loud relative to the drums. I hope I can fix that in the mix."

Lizzi had detonated "Firewall" with a sizzling razzma-tazz on the cymbals; on "Sign of Design," he kept playing after the song ended, adding his own spirited coda. Lizzi wasn't shy on drums. I was glad he wasn't.

AN OCEANIC FEELING-TONE

I T WAS THE END of the day, the time of summer I like best, with a backlit glow from the fading sun. I found myself feeling especially serene as I walked along Sherbrooke, passing the Starbucks where I'd met both Morey and Jo by happenstance, and continuing past the NextDoor Pub, where I'd first fantasized about getting Shaharah to sing "Another Man's Crime." I felt at one with my songs, finally, no anguish over unfinished choruses or clunky bridges or confusion over singers. Most of the plan seemed to be in place now, come what may. Eleven songs were in various stages of completion.

It was a light-at-end-of-tunnel sensation. I felt grateful that I'd met both Morey and Jo. The world that surrounded me seemed like a loving realm. Magic hour with its lyrical lighting had this effect. Bodies of water would do the same trick. I was far from any Zen waterfalls, but an oceanic feeling-tone engulfed me.

On a whim, I texted Jo for the first time in a while. "Hope you're musically happy."

She replied: "??"

I realized that my text must have sounded cryptic. An explanation was in order.

"I'm in a wistful but good mood. I'm at peace with music and hope you are too."

I didn't hear back from her until the next day, and we made plans to have a drink on Avenue du Parc, the main drag of the Mile End neighbourhood, indie-music mecca of the city. Wearing an uncharacteristic downcast expression, a peasant dress, and sandals, she spoke of musical frustration. Although she'd started pitching five songs to record companies and publishers, she was being studiously ignored. I shared my latest notions of the music business (courtesy of Morey) with her.

We walked over to St. Laurent Boulevard, hipster spinal cord of the city, for a glass of white wine and a sandwich. Neither were very tasty. We then walked along upscale Laurier back to Parc and ordered a beer on the *terrasse* of the moment, Buvette chez Simone.

It was a hot, hazy day, cloaked in a pavement-grey sky. I told Jo that she should be proud of what she'd accomplished, that we should both be proud. When we'd met, little more than a year earlier, she didn't even own a keyboard and had no songs to speak of, beyond one dated tune that didn't do her talent justice. My songs were in various states of disrepair at the time, and I was desperate to finish them.

I reminded her that we'd both worked hard on our respective songs and helped each other, she helping me more than vice versa, though it was me who'd spurred her on with her own tunes. Many an early morning we'd emailed each other compositions hot off the press. What works here? What doesn't? A thumbs-up text went a long way towards boosting confidence on the insecure terrain of songwriting. It hadn't been easy; it would have been easier to watch television or do any number of other slacker endeavours. But then we'd have ended up on deathbeds at some point in the future, thinking: *There were songs somewhere inside of me and I never got around to getting them out.* That regret would never happen now. Other regrets, but not this one.

"Something will happen with your songs," I told her. "I don't know how or when, but something will happen."

I walked her to her parked car and told her I was grateful that we'd met. It almost hadn't happened. We'd crossed paths by accident, and only met because I was attracted to a woman in a red knit cap at the table one over from me at a café, and struck up a conversation.

"Thanks for, um, all the harmonious support you've given me," I said.

She hugged me and we said goodbye.

As I walked up Parc, I checked the emails on my phone. One had rolled in from Morey.

Ok, pull up a chair, pour yourself the beverage of your choice, turn out the lights, and get ready to be swept into the madness of my lab. Here is a rough mix of "Honey from the Sky," be prepared to be on the verge of seizure or disbelief, but by the 4th or 5th listen hopefully you should be able to distance yourself from the original and enter my warped sonic vision ... try to listen with headphones if possible (or

a good system) since there are some sounds (electronic bass drum for example) that don't reproduce
on a desktop computer... anyway, here goes, I'm
a bit nervous about this but anxious to hear your
comments.

HONEY FROM THE ATTIC

WHAT I HEARD AT first were four measures of hypnotic kick drum and snare, followed by cloak-and-dagger guitar chords, one strum of espionage per measure, and then strings falling like street-lamp shadows. Hayley's gentle voice entered the stark canvas: *I carried you / every step of the way / loving moves / feet of clay.* In the second part of the verse, Hayley's singing was echoed every other line with a lo-fi double, a black-and-white negative of the colour photo that was her lead vocal.

It was a feeling unlike anything I'd ever experienced—to listen to a song that I had composed unfolding in strange directions. Intensely familiar yet totally strange.

But nothing could prepare me for the shock that was the chorus. The intro and verse had coolly traversed a desolate terrain. Then, two beats—kick drum and snare— unleashed a tidal wave of distortion and mayhem. Churning in the onslaught were jaunty snare rolls and James Bond horns. It was stunning. And then the pendulum swung back from bombast to spaciousness.

Back and forth it went. I immediately loved the creation and emailed Morey my delight even before I got home. I praised his version to the moon: "A fantastic imaginative reworking with Hayley sounding breathtakingly superb."

"I'm relieved," he emailed back.

Inevitably I had some suggestions. I thought the cyclone of a chorus should be toned down to give more room to the vocals, the strings, and the snare drum. And there was a certain degree of sameness running through the song; perhaps a bridge or a solo break would enliven the production.

Morey replied that he'd tone down the power chords in the chorus a bit. But it was clear that he liked the mayhem of it all. He'd apparently tried a solo break and my (unused) bridge, but that made the song too long; it was already clocking in at 4:30.

I also suggested he might wrap some guitar soloing around the last verse, for variety's sake. He later added it, though some of the lines, I felt, could be less bluesy.

He was never going to let me into his "lab" to work on a mix, now that he saw how micromanagerial I could be. But perhaps I was missing the point. I had given him carte blanche with the song. This was his vision. And a glorious vision it was.

IT SEEMED SOMEHOW appropriate that he emailed me the song just as I was telling Jo on Avenue du Parc how I was at peace with music and how I was grateful to her and that I still believed something would come of her singular talent.

That evening I emailed her the Richman rendition of "Honey." She did not reply that night or for a long time the next morning. Finally, she texted me:

J: Holy shit!!!!!!!!

I sought more details.

E: Good shit or bad shit?

J: Great shit!

She also confided that she was blown away by Morey's work and as a result "totally discouraged." It made her feel that her own recordings were stuck in some classic rock mould.

J: My best song sounds like shit compared to what I just heard.

I had to talk her down from the ledge.

E: Your voice and songs are so good that they don't need production bells and whistles. Just voice and piano are enough. Especially if it's a publishing deal you're after.

That referred to Jo's oft-stated desire to sell her songs to a music publisher, as opposed to recording tracks that would end up on an album of her own. But she was unconvinced.

J: Thinking of taking a job at Starbucks.

E: For the record, everyone I play your singing to is in awe of your voice.

J: And yet, when I hear Hayley I feel like a fucken drunken housewife at a karaoke bar.

This was unfortunate, because after many years of an on-again, off-again relationship with music, Jo was just hitting her stride. I regretted ever having emailed her Morey's version of "Honey."

"I had a renaissance," she told me a few days later, "but I'm on the precipice again, in danger of abandoning."

MEANWHILE, MOREY SENT me a surprising email. After stating that he'd tweaked the song further, incorporating some of my suggestions, he said he was happy with the results. He added:

So … would you like to do anything with it in terms of a co-operative effort? Would you have any objections with me using it for Hayley's sites and even possibly a quick video? Credits to Siblin/Richman for writing?

The reference to a shared songwriting credit threw me. Wasn't it still—despite Morey's radical reworking—my composition? I tried to imagine what reason there might be to keep Morey's version under wraps until (and if) I managed to release my own record. I couldn't think of any reason. That settled that. As for the songwriting credit, I was conflicted. But as Morey had recently informed me, "Nobody buys records anymore." It's not as if I was going to be losing a major revenue stream. And Morey had transformed the song. I was appreciative of all the time he and Hayley had put into it, free of charge. Besides, this would mark the first time a song of mine was ever actually going up for sale, albeit not in a record store but on the Internet. The price tag would be ninety-nine cents.

DIONYSIAN BRASS PARADE

T HE HEAT AND HUMIDITY finally abated, leaving the city with a standard-issue hot summer. That came on the heels of a sauna-grade steam bath and an Aztec sun demanding sacrifices of the flesh. I had started to feel like a resident of an intensely southern clime, venturing out only in the early morning or evenings.

There had been no summer getaway for me. Instead my disposable income, was going to studio time, keyboardists, horn players, bassists, drummers, and other air vibrators for hire. Rather than a road trip or seaside vacation, I passed some time with keyboards played by Ralph Télémaque, who squeezed his considerable frame and talent into Krantzberg's chair and played some intricate piano on "Sign of Design."

My old bandmate Michael Leon, a college history prof now, lent his vocals for a remix of "Another Man's Crime." Shaharah's version of that song, while excellent in its own way, continued to feel like a square peg jammed into a round hole. The song was not in her key, as she'd pointed out from the get-go. And now with her vocals so magnificently on display in "Firewall" and "Sign of Design," it seemed like a good idea to diversify the singer star power. Maybe, as Jo said, it was a male vocal song after all. The title suggested as much, and Leon possessed a unique singing voice redolent of something Celtic, possibly an atavistic legacy of his father's childhood in Dublin.

There was also need for guitar solos. Rather than call in favours, twist arms, or pay cash, it was one area where I could DIY. If I lined up specialists to play everything from soups to nuts, what of my singer-songwriter DNA would remain in the songs? So I worked on it daily with my Gibson L6, trying to fill harmonic holes for several songs. With most of my friends and musical collaborators decamped to seaside getaways or cottage country, I had plenty of time to hunker down with my electric guitar and devise solos. The results were unpromising at first, but as I played and played and noodled and noodled, often with my Zoom personal assistant, I slowly made progress.

The songs were suddenly falling into place. It was mostly icing on the cake that was missing—a few instruments that would add texture and provide solos. And brass was the richest of ingredients that I imagined adding. I had zero experience with horn sections but could hear them in a few places. The most obvious home for brass was on "Go Slow," a tune for which I'd long envisioned a trumpet hook. Perhaps it was the New Orleans setting of the song, which lamented Ian Crystal's tragic death. References in the verses to a "Dionysian brass parade" and "victories cast in bronze" summoned both horns and the antiquity in which Ian was an expert.

Bilerman had given me the name of trumpeter Ellwood Epps (a good name at that), and I emailed him a rough draft of "Go Slow" along with the ersatz trumpet part Krantzberg and I had slapped together with the MIDI controller.

Ellwood Epps showed up at Hotel2Tango with a black case that held his trumpet, and vertically pointed hair that looked as if he'd run his fingers through it. A gregarious man who looked to be in his late thirties, Epps is one of the city's foremost trumpet improvisers. The many bands he's played in include Land of Marigold, the Ratchet Orchestra, Pink Saliva, and Stuffy Turkey, the latter devoted exclusively to the music of Thelonious Monk. A major part of his career has been directing both the L'envers and the Mardi Spaghetti series of improvised music concerts in the Mile End neighbourhood.

A mic was set up for Epps and his trumpet, and we were soon into the song. He did a few takes, and during one of them I went off to use the bathroom, separated from the studio proper by a heavy door. I waited before going back into the recording room because through the small window in the door I could see Epps — it was a poetic sight to watch him playing his golden instrument against the crimson backdrop of the big curtain that sections off the tracking room. When he finished his performance, I went back in. That was the take we kept.

I later took great pleasure in adding some cello to the songs. While listening to the "band version" of "Cherries," I had the idea of making an acoustic version. Cello came to mind, and Bilerman put me in touch with Kristina Koropecki, who plays with the singer Mark Berube. Koropecki laid down a beguiling cello solo for "Cherries," weaving in flowing, lyrical lines to what had become a sparse, minimalist song. She did it in no time, so I asked her to play a bit on "Grace of Love," which she also did with engaging results.

Eli Krantzberg, meanwhile, had been busy. He'd been on a well-deserved vacation for two weeks in Vermont with Mariam. While there, he learned that the Logic recording system was upgrading its software, a major development tantamount to the redesign of a car model. The last time it had happened was four years ago. Krantzberg knew he'd have to quickly figure out the upgrade and produce an instructional video pronto.

When he got back home, he headed to the basement pretty well right away and applied himself to the new software. Plus there were imminent upgrades to other software. As Morey once told me, to master just one of the digital audio workstations like Logic, Pro Tools, or Cubase is an incredibly challenging amount of work and aptitude. "And Eli has mastered several of them."

At Studio K., we added some brass to "Firewall." Saxophonist Erik Hove, all six feet five inches of him, crammed into Krantzberg's basement. Dressed entirely in black save for white sneakers, he wore a neatly trimmed beard and rectangular glasses. He brought all the skills of a prize-winning alto saxophonist who has played improvised music, indie pop, hip-hop, and "Balkan groove," as well as experimental turntable jazz in the group Soundclash.

As Hove warmed up his sax, I marvelled at the flashy instrument. It looked quite machine-like — not surprisingly, I remarked, as it was only invented in the nineteenth century. "The inventor's name was Sax, no?

"Adolphe Sax," he told me.

"Good thing they didn't name the instrument an adol-phone," I said.

"Ha!"

"You'd be known as an adolphonist."

It didn't take Hove long to lay down a brilliant tenor solo, channelling both the raw power and the sophisticated glitz of the instrument.

Whereas the violin brings to mind handcrafted artisan-ship, the burnished metal of a sax suggests factory pro-duction. Its look is that of an old typewriter fused with an Edison phonograph. Yet its basic shape it is much older, as pastoral and biblical as a ram's horn.

Packing up his instrument, Hove told me that despite its factory-built sheen, every saxophone sounds very different, in that some of its keys resonate better than others.

"There is nothing cookie-cutter about it," he said. "It's very hard to create synthetic sax sounds."

I had captured some high-end material for the songs. Hove had played what was probably the most blistering, virtuosic solo to appear on any of my songs. And I had great trouble imagining that a computer could ever come up with something quite so compelling.

ZEROS AND ONES WITH
A HUMAN FACE

"YOU HAVE TO MANUALLY input the sloppiness."

We were in Morey's home office because the desktop computer there provided a bigger display than his laptop upstairs in the attic studio. The office is handsomely appointed, with a fireplace, oriental throw rugs, and crimson walls. The south window admits a great deal of sunshine. The two of us were seated on hard-backed wood chairs facing the big screen of an iMac. As promised, Morey was walking me through his computer-based recording of "Honey from the Sky."

"Let's take it from the very beginning," I said. "What did you first start working on?"

"I did a whole version of the song that was just like yours," he said. "But I was never truly happy with it, because it wasn't very original." The first thing he'd imagined to make it original was a pounding crash cymbal on the chorus.

He'd also recalled my suggestion that he give the song a "trip-hop" makeover along the lines of bands I have a soft spot for, like Massive Attack, Portishead, and Morcheeba.

The crash of a cymbal suggested to Morey how the verse and chorus could be very different creatures. With that dichotomy in mind, he quickly "breezed through the song." Yet the work he'd done did not look like a breeze to me. Up on the screen were all the tracks he'd used for "Honey" — and all the ones he experimented with and rejected. The unused tracks numbered more than 150.

Morey began deconstructing the song for me note for note. Most of those notes, he explained, were in fact digital commands — samples — stored in his computer. With the exception of Hayley's singing and his guitar playing, the instrument sounds he used were all computer-generated.

"But they're all very authentic sounds," he said. "They're all real samples. They all sound great." They had indeed ended up sounding great in Morey's soundscape, but only after much tinkering, massaging, and colouring.

"Show me one of the sounds in detail," I asked him.

The first track he singled out was a lone violin, a sample that he "triggered" on his MIDI keyboard controller. When he isolated that single violin and we gave it a listen, it sounded pretty crappy to me. But when doubled with a second violin, using a slight "delay," suddenly it all sounded very credible.

To build a string part and find the string sounds that he ended up keeping, various combinations involving violins and violas were tried, tested, and rejected. Interestingly, Morey said that after coming up with the violin line, he'd become anxious that he might have unconsciously lifted it from some famous melody. An old Jewish melody is what he suspected, going back maybe a couple of hundred years. Or something ethnic—Egyptian, possibly. He researched as best he could on the Internet but found nothing. To this day he thinks that the melody must exist somewhere other than in "Honey from the Sky."

Morey then dissected the main electric guitar track used on the song. A real instrument, this one: he had played the guitar. Nonetheless, much computer soundscaping happened with this sound as well.

One individual track was labelled "Brownface Crunch Verb." I asked what the heck it was. "Brownface," he told me, referred to a Fender guitar amp of the same name, and "Verb" is short for reverb. "Crunch" was pretty self-explanatory. Morey had selected the Fender Brownface sound from hundreds of "amp modules" (computer-based recreations of actual amplifiers). And within this amp module, he micromanaged three subcategories of sound— cabinet type, microphone type, and mic placement—as precisely as if he were using the real McCoys in-studio. In addition, he selected any effects he might desire from the virtual Pedalboard, which offers a multicoloured array of effects pedals, such as Monster Fuzz.

More sound parameters were adjusted in Channel EQ, such as the impressively named Tweedy Goodness (which lives up to its appellation). Morey showed how he "shelved off some low end" of the EQ and tweaked it in other ways. Finally, he doubled that track with "a little delay," as he did for the violins.

"What's with this bit of delay being used?" I wanted to know. "What does it really do?"

"If everything is played at exactly the same time, it would sound stiff," Morey said. That is to say it would sound like a machine, not like a human being. The slight delay of one part overlapping another, identical part gives it a human touch, as well as some thickness in texture.

Programming the human touch is a challenge. That's not a problem when Morey the human being is playing guitar, but when he programs an instrument like bass from sampled computer sounds, it's another story. "You have to manually input the sloppiness," he said. To that end, Morey showed me how he placed each individual tone of his bassline "a little off, like a real player. If you didn't do that, it wouldn't sound real."

He used the computer mouse to move those bass tones a little ahead of or a bit behind the beat. This altered the timing, making it less than perfect. (It reminded me of Shaharah's bassist, Greg Provo, and how his subtle timing of note placement made what he was doing so terrific; and also how producer Don Was celebrated the slight rhythmic differences of the musicians in a band like the Rolling Stones.)

This is a big challenge for many music programmers, especially those who do not play guitar. "It's not a perfect instrument, you don't tune it perfectly, and you don't play it perfectly," said Morey. Therefore if you're going to program guitar into music you have to take pains to make it less than perfect. "Luckily, I play guitar."

Morey did the same thing for countless other instruments. "Everything is a little off," he explained. The sole exception was the bass drum, "the heartbeat of the song." But even that instrument, which kicked off the song in thumping, hypnotic fashion, was altered volume-wise here and there to render it more human.

We made our way through the timeline of the song to the chorus. For a lingering couple of seconds, there's that silent space.

"Nothing," said Morey, pausing the music. His blue eyes lit up. "Then this."

The explosion that is the chorus detonated.

For the chorus, Morey added other tracks: two more string sections, electric guitar, a rolling snare drum, and bass guitar (which — surprisingly, to me — appears only in the choruses). Backup vocal harmonies were also massaged into the mix.

"How many tracks in total did you use for the song?" I asked.

Morey had to count them — the number was twenty-five. Some of the instruments, such as the organ sound ("Deep Purple") on the third chorus, were inaudible to me before he singled them out.

What's more, I came to realize, all those sampled instrument sounds he was using were infinitely changeable. To make that point, Morey took the violin part and, with a flick of his mouse, turned it into Steinway piano. Same musical line, different instrument. From there he converted it into a flute.

"How about a funk horn section?" I suggested.

Done.

"They're all zeros and ones," he said.

But zeros and ones with a human face. Morey tried hard to make those computer sounds as human as possible. He did it, as I now knew, by pushing the sounds around the beat so that they were not too perfect, not too robotic. He also employed a nifty plug-in: the Humanizer!

On the Logic recording system that he used, there was an effect function called Humanizer which tried to do just that. It actually inserted tiny variations in the performance of a given instrument (more specifically, variations in the volume, placement, and length of any one note). And the programmer could determine just how much variation (i.e., humanity) was wanted. Morey would decide, for example, to have a particular sound "humanized" randomly by, say, 5 or 10 percent. It had to be tailored to the attack of the instrument in question. He did it all over the place, except for the guitar that he actually played, and for Hayley's voice, both of which were sufficiently human.

He might also alter the tempo of the song in places — the beats per minute, which human musicians do not play with absolute perfection. This was why the famous, or infamous, click track was such a sensitive issue among musicians. It meant playing to an ironclad (and hence not very human) metronome.

In my experience it sometimes worked, sometimes not. "When I was recording 'Achilles' at Hotel2Tango," I told Morey, "we used a click. But after a while, when the energy of the song intensfied, I found that the click was forcing Bucky, Morgan, and me to march in lockstep. I asked Bilerman whether he could remove the click towards the end of the song, when we needed to let loose. I think it helped humanize matters."

Morey agreed, and said that if he were to make an actual record today, as opposed to YouTube videos, he would spend much more time altering the BPMs throughout the song. (In fact he'd spend a lot more time with everything. It took him about a day or two to create one of his songs. If a record was the aim, he would spend a month "getting it right.")

But it all depended on the sort of music you were making. For electronic music or pop hits, perfect timing might be the perfect recipe. To illustrate his point, Morey opened up iTunes, and we gave a listen to songs currently in the Top 40. The differences blurred between Britney Spears, Katy Perry, and Lady Gaga.

"What's real in there?" Morey asked. "This is a guy on a laptop," he said about one generic production. "Even the voice is computer-generated. They're not even *trying* to duplicate a real instrument; they're computer instruments. I'm literally trying to do stuff that sounds authentic."

We gave a listen to the Lady Gaga hit du jour. "Think that's a real drum?" He laughed. "The computer is your instrument here."

The trend is not without its worrisome component for Morey. He cited Guitar Hero, the video game that has empowered a generation of ersatz musicians. The idea behind Guitar Hero is to pretend to play. Not actually play. Guide the computer.

"No one likes playing anymore," he said.

Perched atop Morey's iMac monitor was a little plastic Don Quixote–type guitar player. It seemed more real than the sounds coming out of the Top 40.

A WEEK WENT by, and I got to Jonah James early and was reading the Montreal *Gazette*, an Americano in hand, when Morey showed up. He joined me at a *terrasse* table shaded by a sprawling tree. We spoke about the world of newspapers for a long while before he dropped his bombshell. It sounded like a bombshell to me, though he was nonchalant about it.

A few days earlier, Hayley had received an email from a Sony Music exec, saying that he found her YouTube material interesting and could she put him in touch with her father or guardian. Morey was soon exchanging emails with the label's top A&R (Artists & Repertoire) man for Canada. They chatted on the phone. The Sony exec said he liked Hayley's cover songs posted on YouTube, that he appreciated the music's "left-of-centre" quality. Could they meet for lunch sometime? His office was in Toronto, but he'd be in Montreal the following week with two colleagues.

"Wow," I said. "That's big news."

"The question," Morey said, "is what does he want?"

Morey drew a comparison with the sports world. "It's like a fourteen-year-old hockey player who is too young to do anything but who has talent and shows promise... They scout you, follow you, give you little pointers."

"But this has to mean something, no?"

"To take you out for lunch is a bit of a next step," Morey said. Maybe they wanted to sign a "development deal," which could mean Sony contributing a song or two out of their "vaults," maybe getting Hayley in the recording studio, making a demo recording— "and maybe over the next few years something will come of this."

Using an expression that had come up a lot in our chats, he said that for the record company it was like "throwing spaghetti against the wall." They wanted to see what would stick. "Cynical people would call it a slavery deal."

Yet there were success stories that had originated in such

deals. Morey cited the case of the teen singer from New Zealand who goes by the stage name Lorde. She signed a development deal at the age of twelve. In the summer of 2013, at sixteen, she'd topped the iTunes download charts for New Zealand and signed with a major label. "She's on the verge of stardom," he said. (Within months, Lorde would in fact catapult to fame.)

If a major label was interested in Hayley, he figured, it would be with that sort of thing in mind. "Every once in a while they'd give her a carrot. She would be in their stable."

Morey, however, was not your average stage dad, chomping at the bit for a taste of fame. Putting the Sony news aside, he was keen to talk about his latest cover song, a tune by Radiohead that the British band had not yet recorded in the studio. Morey had crafted a tantalizing version of the song, called "Identikit," sung by Hayley, and thrown it on YouTube. It received a barrage of "shares" on Radiohead fan clubs, chat sites, and band forums that encompass maybe eight hundred thousand — count 'em — people. In total, Radiohead probably has somewhere in the neighbourhood of twenty such groups boasting millions of fans. Hayley's item got shared on fifteen of them, resulting in tens of thousands of views. That might not be pasta glued to the wall for Hayley, but it does count as viral.

"What does all this get her?" I asked.

"There's no money, but you can create a fan base; maybe you can turn it into something, maybe not. For people of Hayley's age, music is not something you buy," Morey reminded me.

"What about your original songs?" I asked. "Do you think they're of interest to Sony?" Morey and Hayley had four such tunes posted on the Internet, including "Honey from the Sky."

Morey's guess was that the record label would probably try to muscle in on that territory too. "Say they want 'Honey,'" he continued. "The label would probably say that they have some people in-house for production; they'd fund the recording of the song, send in their own producer, handle all of the promotion and marketing. But—and here's the big but—they would want to wrest control of the publishing rights. Bands used to quickly agree to this arrangement, forgo their publishing rights in exchange for, say, fifty thousand dollars, or to see their name up in lights."

If in fact Sony were to grab publishing rights, Morey's songs would be owned by the largest music publishing company in the world, Sony/ATV, which is jointly owned by Sony Corporation and Michael Jackson's estate. That would be a fun—if not so lucrative—fact for the songwriter.

Morey explained that these rights are technically known as a "mechanical licence" and have their origin a century ago, when player pianos came on the scene. Ever since, the statutory publishing rate has been 8.3 cents per sale of a five-minute song (9.1 cents in the U.S.).

But with no record label in on the action, Morey de facto owned the publishing rights to his songs (nobody in fact had those rights, but he could have easily proven ownership, along with yours truly for "Honey"). That meant he would keep that 8.3 cents per sale, and more. On a ninety-nine-cent sale of a song on iTunes, for example, Morey would make about sixty-five cents for one of his original songs, with the rest going to administrative, placement, and commission fees. If he was signed with a major label, his take would be closer to about ten cents.

Which reminded him: Hayley's four original songs, "Honey" among them, were up for sale on iTunes. After a year of posting YouTube videos of Hayley singing smartly crafted covers, and a month or two after throwing four originals together on artist sites like ReverbNation and Bandcamp, Morey had taken the next step. He put their original songs up for sale on iTunes. He considered it a gift—costing about seventy dollars in various fees—to his daughter.

"Her face lit up," he said, describing how she reacted to the news. "It became such a big deal." This, for a teenager (not to mention for a middle-aged amateur songwriter), is like seeing your name up in lights. "Now that it's on iTunes, it's wow! It's pro . . . If you're on iTunes you're an artist. She's sitting beside (alphabetically, anyways) Radiohead, Portishead, and the Rolling Stones."

Morey and Hayley owned the publishing rights to their songs, but iTunes would take a share, as would CD Baby, which acted as the "agent." That left the Richmans with about 70 percent of sales—not the whole shebang, but a heck of a lot more than the 8.3 cents they would have received if they'd signed away their rights to a major label.

And after being up on iTunes for one week, the father-daughter duo had sold, at ninety-nine cents a song—drum roll, please—nineteen copies. That figure included three people whom Hayley knew, as well as one buyer from the Punjab, India, and another from Ontario. (iTunes provides a weekly "trending" report to its artists that contains this info.) Three of the purchases were for "Honey from the Sky," which meant I should not have bought Morey the coffee I'd sprung for.

CHERRY-PICKING AT
THE HOTEL

THE WAITING LIST WAS always very long to get a session at Hotel2Tango. It was good to be back once again in the big tracking room with the faded oriental rugs and the pink Victorian couch, the walls lined with keyboards, vintage amps, effects pedals, and retro posters. Gone were Bucky and Morgan, and their absence made the room feel cavernous and empty and preternaturally quiet. But the void also contained something meditative.

When I'd recorded with Bucky and Morgan, I'd played guitar and sung at the same time, but those performances were meant to be guide tracks to lead the other musicians through unfamiliar songs. I'd since recorded more polished guitar parts and was working on the vocals.

Bilerman still was of the arguable opinion that I should sing my songs. I was semi-convinced enough to sing a few of them. I'd earlier done a successful version of "Go Slow" but, as things turned out, was not able to improve on the original vocal guide track for "Basement Rainbow." So we kept that track of me singing in real time while playing guitar alongside Bucky and Morgan. An unadorned performance, captured live — Bilerman's ideal.

"Nine times out of ten you're not going to use the vocals sung live with the rest of the band," Bilerman told me. "But as this session has proven, the one time that you do, it's because they're better than anything you can do just with headphones and a microphone. The vocals that we used with you singing with the band are so much more connected to the song, to the spirit of the song, the energy of the song."

Whether this meant my voice was actually better than I'd imagined, or far worse, was not clear. A bit of both, I supposed. Either way, I moved on to "Achilles." As I sang, I looked out onto the cavernous room and focused on the frosted glass bricks in the distance, watching the dappled play of light.

The results seemed all right. But no single version of the five vocal takes of "Achilles" had it all. And so Bilerman and I were now at his computer, more specifically at his Pro Tools digital audio workstation. We were going through the various takes. Every time a line, or even a word, was especially weak, we'd replace it with a better version (if we could find one) from another take. This is what's known in studio parlance as "comping" — creating a composite track by cherry-picking the best bits from multiple takes and piecing them together.

"Sometimes," Bilerman told me, "people say they don't like the *s* at the end of a word." When that happens, he can often splice out the offending *s* and replace it with a better one. Later, he had occasion to show me just that with one of my words.

Given Bilerman's analogue ethos and live-performance MO, I was surprised that he indulged in this sort of digital sleight of hand. But he's flexible. He tailors his work on a song-by-song basis.

Bilerman told me that his views on the computer-versus-tape debate, the analogue-digital divide, had evolved. "The biggest difference between recording to tape and record-ing on a computer is not the way it sounds but the way it makes you work as a musician recording," he said. "If you're recording on tape you have a limited number of tracks—in our case we have a 24-track machine—so at a certain point you cannot overdub anymore. It forces you to assess what's important and what's superfluous, whereas with a computer there's way too much superfluous stuff because there is no cutoff, no limitation."

The upshot: limitations raise the stakes in the studio and force musicians to focus with an intensity akin to a live performance. Playing in the here and now, as opposed to postponing decisions (and infinite overdubs), makes for better records, Bilerman said.

I saw his point. But it seemed to me that the digital genie was out of the bottle, making it all too tempting with a recording system like Pro Tools to do things such as replace an *s* in one of my vocal lines or grab the best parts of five performances and stitch them together into one. (Perhaps the ideal is what I'd in fact been doing at H2T: live bed tracks that provided the core of performance followed up with some modest overdubbing and digital editing.)

Truth be told, engineers of yesteryear could also do this

sort of thing with magnetic tape, but it was far more time-consuming, difficult, and costly.

Hotel2Tango still offers the possibility of recording on magnetic tape instead of digital. Ten reels will set you back about $3,500. To get an idea of how much tape is used, I went through the equivalent of one reel (thirty-three minutes, which is approximately eight versions of the song) trying to nail "Basement Rainbow." Does the aspiring artist prefer to spend three thousand dollars on eight reels of tape or on forty hours of studio time? Analogue fetishism and big budgets aside, the answer seems pretty obvious.

Bilerman explained that there are really three components of sound recording, each with both digital and analogue versions. First of all, there is the recording system: either a magnetic tape machine or a digital audio workstation. Second: effects—either "outboard gear," machines the size of stereo receivers, rack-mounted and stacked atop one another; or virtual plug-in versions, located in the computer. Third is the mixer—either an analogue console with its vast acreage of faders and knobs and meters, which defined the look of a recording studio over the past several decades, or a virtual mixer in the computer.

Until a few years earlier, Hotel2Tango had not even had a computer. Now the studio had a hybrid system and was still known for its analogue philosophy and gear. All the physical equipment was there, but so were its digital incarnations.

In my case, Bilerman explained, we were recording and playing back in the digital world (albeit using analogue instruments, amps, and the real-life sound of the studio room), we would manipulate those sounds in the analogue world with effects from outboard gear, and the mixing would be analogue, with Bilerman working the faders and knobs of his big console.

Seven songs of mine were now in varying stages of completion at Hotel2Tango. Bilerman suggested that we do one more batch of sessions to finish recording and then do the mix. That seemed over-optimistic to me. But I'd made progress and could now contemplate a day when I would have what is still called a record.

MAJOR HANDCUFFS

A S I HEADED INTO the final stretch of crafting the songs, a singer on one of them was being courted by top Sony Music brass.

Hayley Richman was trembling with nerves when she and her dad stepped from the cobblestone streets of Old Montreal into Le Muscadin, a pricey Italian restaurant with tuxedoed waiters and a highly regarded wine cellar.

Morey told me that once inside, he and Hayley joined three Sony higher-ups: the A&R chief for Canada, a promotions director, and a department head. Over lunch, they learned that it was on account of Internet misinformation that the A&R man had gotten wind of Hayley.

The error was the Lana Del Rey cover that had gone viral on the mistaken perception that it was an actual Del Rey performance. The Sony exec had been cruising the net when he came across the song and the ensuing kerfuffle (which was only cleared up when Hayley posted that it was she — a fourteen-year-old kid in Quebec — who'd performed the song).

From there, the Sony man went to Hayley's YouTube channel and was attracted by the fact that many of his favourite bands — Radiohead and Portishead among them — were being covered so well by a kid. Everyone in his Toronto office became intrigued with the young singer.

The Sony exec suggested he was interested in doing a development deal of some sort. "But he was very coy," Morey recalled. "It ended up with Sony saying that they're very interested, that they'd like to pursue this further. They said they're going to go back to the office, mull things over, and send us a development proposal."

Which was what? Morey knew exactly what. Sony would likely throw them a few bones, nothing very costly, perhaps offer to record a demo with their own musicians, producer, and songwriters, and would promise to "use their expertise and guidance to direct where this might go in the future."

In a word — "babysit."

And in exchange for being treated like pasta with potential, Hayley would be expected to sign an exclusive deal with Sony for a number of years. She'd be handcuffed to the major label. Shackles, it must be said, that most teenagers singing covers on YouTube would be very happy to wear.

"They were a little more interested than I thought they'd be," Morey said.

"What about your original songs?" I asked.

"They never mentioned the original songs, or whether she wrote songs," Morey said. "It was almost as if they didn't know they existed."

One interpretation is that Sony didn't stand to make all

that much money from a Richman original tune. Whereas Morey and Hayley owned their own songs, Sony would profit much more from songs they already had in their own vault. The label would be more inclined to connect one of its producers (someone already under contract, maybe) with its own songwriters, musicians, studios, and so on. There was little room in this model for original songs by a fourteen-year-old kid and her dad.

I suppose if Morey wrote an incredibly infectious pop song like "MMMBop" or "Rehab," they'd take notice. But even then, perhaps only if it spread like wildfire on the web.

Which in today's day and age may be the point. Coincidentally, Sony UK (no connection with Sony Canada's courtship) got in touch with Hayley to ask whether her cover of a Kodaline song could be included in a collection the Irish rock band was putting together of its favourite covers of its own material. This thrilled Hayley to no end.

And then a company making beauty videos asked permission from Hayley to use another of her covers — yet another Lana Del Rey song, "Young and Beautiful." Within a few weeks, the beauty video generated some ten thousand views, three hundred new subscribers to Hayley's YouTube channel, upwards of 150 comments, and a dozen requests to use her covers for other beauty videos.

Yet there was an ethical wrinkle. "The sad thing," Morey told me, "is that the songwriter is not getting compensated. It does something for Hayley, but I sort of have a moral-ethical conflict about this. Does it translate into more sales and interest for the original song? Maybe. But there's definitely an exploitation factor."

The publisher of the song could always take the cover

down from the Internet. "They do take things down, but they cherry-pick... YouTube is one big copyright loophole."

Morey knows about this sort of thing. When he ran his record company, he did an album of Halloween songs and—stretching the concept a bit—included a cover of the Bruce Springsteen tune "Dead Man Walkin'." A letter from Springsteen's agent arrived, complaining about the use of the song on such a record. The Halloween context allegedly "changed the character of the song," which is something you need permission to do. The song was dropped from the album.

Hayley, meanwhile, had thoroughly enjoyed being courted by a major label. "She liked the celebrity treatment," her dad said. Band members from Simple Minds walked into the restaurant at one point. The Sony guy offered to get Hayley some backstage passes for bands she liked. Yet it didn't go to her head.

"She thought it was a great experience. She didn't feel, 'Oh, I'm going to make it!' I think she's more realistic. It wasn't like, 'I can quit school now.' But it was a good experience for her. She got to see what it's like on the other side of the table."

They were waiting to hear what Sony had to say, though Morey wasn't holding his breath. "I don't know what they're going to do next."

POMEGRANATE SEEDS

I'M NOT SAYING THAT Jo is a diva, but her early-morning shopping list made me think as much. Pomegranate seeds, papaya, and a bottle of sparkling water. She had agreed to sing a song at Hotel2Tango. Given her busy life and general skill for cancelling on me at the last minute, I was happy to chase down pomegranate seeds if it meant getting her capricious ass into studio gear.

She was going to sing "Cherries." Early in the morning she'd texted me asking for the lyrics. She texted back:

J: It's hard for me to get through the song. It makes me think of dad and I get all choked up.

I reminded her who the song is about:

E: Think of my grandfather!

J: *I swear I'm afraid I will break down.*

E: *Emotion is good. That's what makes you a fab singer.*

J: *Ya, but actually crying is not the best.*

E: *Modern recording. We do as many takes as necessary. Cut and paste if need be. Airbrush the tears.*

I then told her that I was off to buy some snacks for the session. Did she want anything?

J: *Chips and beer . . . Kidding. Papaya and or pomegranate seeds would be great. And Perrier or something.*

Two stores later, I complained about her operatic demands. She did not modify her requests.

J: *Don't forget the black truffle oil for me to rub on my elbows. Can't sing with chapped elbows.*

E: *Here I was thinking a homemade peanut butter sandwich would suffice.*

J: *Will make me phlegmy!*

I arrived at Hotel2Tango a bit before Jo, carrying my Gibson and a knapsack containing, among other things, the pomegranate seeds. She turned up soon afterwards, and Bilerman wasted no time in setting up the right mic for her. She applied her voice to "Cherries" and it melted into the song like butter on a fresh croissant. This would put to rest any notion Bilerman had of my voice being best for my songs. Jo then added some backups.

Determined to milk as much pro bono skill out of her as I could, I then asked if she would consider singing backup on another song. She seemed to be having a good time; the big recording room at Hotel2Tango, with its cluttered analogue aura and faded grandeur, must have appealed to her.

Jo laced the choruses of "Go Slow," "Basement Rainbow," and "Perfect Shell" with mellifluous harmonies. In the process, some unscripted ideas were sparked. She delayed the timing of one of the chorus lines in "Basement Rainbow" so that it echoed my vocals — a nifty touch. She was working hard, and I had to urge her to take a break for papaya and pomegranate seeds. Towards the end of "Perfect Shell," she came up with a frothy little phrase in the spirit of Bacharach. Then she had to rush off to pick her son up from school.

After Jo left, I went to work on the final lead vocals on "Perfect Shell." This was the vocal-accident song for me, the one I'd intended as a countrified tune that Rebecca Campbell would sing. To recap: I had transposed it to her key, which had forced me to sing falsetto on the bed track, provoking ribbing from Morgan and Bucky; in retaliation, I'd switched to a low speaking-style voice, and they'd surprised me by urging me to sing it that way.

My arm serendipitously twisted, I was now trying to recreate that tentative vocal I'd done for the bed tracks. It was not so easy. Bilerman gave me a revolutionary suggestion that helped a great deal: he told me to remove the headphones from one ear so I could better hear myself. It was a godsend.

Bilerman was working hard to get my voice to succeed. He pointed out a fire-engine-red gizmo (tube vocal pre-amp) and explained that it was his most expensive recent purchase. It looked like a contemporary remake of a vintage piece of gear, which is exactly what it was.

My voice was going through it, Bilerman explained. Then he blended my last two vocal takes, doubling them, which gave my pipes a smoother, thicker texture. At the rock bottom of the register, and rubbing up against Jo's angelic backups, my baritone sounded as if it could use some Prozac.

I made a sandwich run to a Vietnamese joint on Avenue Bernard, and we broke for a quick bite, discussing draconian clauses in recording contracts while Gus the studio dog roamed free.

I had some electric guitar tracks to add, and got organized only to discover that my guitar pick had gone missing. Guitar picks and nine-volt batteries disappear pretty quickly in the studio, I learned. (Unlike less practical items—like, for example, pricey sunglasses, which I was told would still be waiting for you at H2T in the same spot three months after you forgot them there.) I managed to find a yellow pick in the control room and made do with it, even if the extra-hard gauge was not ideal.

I was also hoping Jo might return. I had texted her my thanks for her productivity earlier and asked whether we might see her back to play some keyboards. All she needed, it turned out, was the right incentive.

J: I may be persuaded to return if there were a couple of cans of Stella Artois waiting in the fridge . . .

Around dinnertime, Jo showed. She had mentioned days before that she'd come up with a little keyboard part for "Cherries," and I was curious to hear it. The piano at the studio, however, had very high action and was hard to play, so Bilerman and I carried an electronic keyboard into the control room. We set it up on the coffee table by the black couch.

We experimented with various sounds and opted for organ. Jo played her little line, which turned out to be a bona fide solo, and we were all pretty charmed with the results. It was an expertly composed solo. She then obliged with some atmospheric organ chords (known as "pads") over the rest of the song.

Eager to get more of her keyboards into my jukebox, I convinced her to try her hand at more organ pads for other songs. I had placed the sheet music over the keyboard and she was reading as she went along. One defective key kept getting stuck, emitting a low drone. We tried various remedies until Bilerman placed an old-fashioned pencil eraser under the key.

No headphones were necessary, because she was recording direct (no mics) into the computer. I sat on the couch next to her. Gus padded around. It was the first time I'd recorded in the small control room, and it felt pleasantly relaxed and cozy.

In many ways my whole music-reawakening eighteen months or so earlier had revolved around Jo's singing and her smart feedback on my songs. I had very much wanted to form a band with her, or at least have her do all the singing. But she balked. She reacted by purchasing an electric keyboard and throwing herself into her own songwriting.

Her absence from my project over the past months was understandable; she was a talented pianist, wrote her own material, and had the benefit of a voice that ennobled whatever tune it sang.

But now, after a fashion, we'd come full circle, and she was singing and playing on several of my songs, as I'd so wanted. As Jo cycled through one song after the other, sitting on the couch, playing organ, I couldn't resist whispering: "You've finally joined my band!"

A TUNEFUL SIGH

I'VE BEEN IN THREE bands worth remembering: Cloudburst, Wet Paint, and a mid-1990s band that played only originals and performed only once, at a loft party on St. Laurent, above the restaurant Bagel Etc. I remember the chatter of the audience drowning out the music, and the fact that someone stole my cassette player.

This band was led by myself and Michael Leon. We each wrote songs and sang the ones we wrote. His material was far better than mine. I wanted to name the band Coin Toss for Water, a name he vetoed. He wanted to name the band Dogfish, which I would have no part of. We remained nameless. Along with a couple of other musicians, we recorded songs on an eight-track tape reel-to-reel machine.

The band broke up when Michael Leon's marriage dissolved and he left town. Years later, when he was teaching history at Dawson College, we reconnected. Leon, by now remarried, was in a power pop band with his theatre director wife, Emma Tibaldo. They even had a name—the Tibaldos. Once in a while I'd jam with Leon and was hoping to involve him in my current project. I wanted to ask whether he'd play his accordion on "Basement Rainbow." But his father had just died in Prince Edward Island, and I feared it might be too soon to ask for a musical favour.

Having the accordion on "Basement" seemed appropriate. When Leon left town all those years ago, he'd also left behind his accordion in my basement apartment on Rue Ste-Famille. It looked like a piece of red Mustang convertible. Now and then I would accidentally brush against it and the instrument would emit a tuneful sigh, as if expressing its unhappiness about the breakup of the band, the end of a marriage, and its owner's disappearance. I started to write a song with the image of Leon and a suitcase in mind. The street was slanted, the sky gunmetal grey, and he was saying goodbye to everything.

I emailed Leon and apologized if the timing was inappropriate. Would he play accordion on this one tune at Hotel-2Tango? To my delight, he agreed. I picked him up at his home in Griffintown, just south of the downtown core, a neighbourhood making the transition from gritty to gentrified. Leon was waiting on the sidewalk, wearing jeans, a grey T-shirt, and a thin beard. He got into my car, lugging his old accordion in its black case.

At Hotel2Tango, Bilerman set up a mic for the accordion in the tracking room and Leon strapped on the ruby-red instrument with keys on one side and buttons on the other. It didn't take him more than a couple of takes to weave his understated, tasteful lines into the ballad.

The tune that was once inspired by Leon and his accordion now felt existentially complete. As it hadn't taken very long, and knowing that Leon is a gifted multi-instrumentalist, I asked whether he might do some more playing. The keyboard that Jo had used was still sitting on the coffee table in the control room, and Leon got behind it. Bilerman cued up "Achilles," and my old friend effortlessly laid down a solid organ track.

Gus was meandering around the room, so I massaged his aging coat to keep him in place and forestall any canine interruptions. (On one occasion, Bilerman had told me, Gus barked during the tracking of a Vic Chesnutt album. The bark made it onto the record.)

While patting the dog, I studied the rack-mounted outboard gear lined against one wall—colourful decks with names like Space Echo, Effectron, Distressor, Dyna-Mite, Teletronix, Transient Designer, and Tube Head. I remembered meeting Bilerman in the control room six months earlier and being awed by the equipment.

The organ take done, Leon graciously agreed to sing backups on "Achilles." As former history classmates, we cracked jokes about Gus the dog, referring to him as Octavian (the Roman Emperor Augustus's original name). And when Leon sang the chorus, I suggested that the word "centuries" be elongated to match my vocals.

"The centuries tend to drag out," I said.

Leon smiled. "Indeed they do."

That was about all the free labour I could extract from my one-time bandmate, who left to catch the fabled 80 bus southbound on Avenue du Parc. He had a digital recorder and was planning to capture some audio for a soundscape he was putting together for a theatre production. The play was set on a bus.

Now I was alone in the studio with the clock winding down. This was supposed to be my last "tracking" day, the final recording session. (At a later date there would be mixing to do, a crucial last stage in the process, which Bilerman would carry out.) I had asked Morey to swing by in order to play some lead guitar, though he was iffy about whether he could make it. I'd also invited Jo to pop by. But for the moment they were no-shows.

My vocals, as usual, required some work. In the big room, yet again singing into the mic, I was asked by Bilerman to double and then triple the lead vocals for "Achilles." The aim was to thicken them. While he squished the various takes together I walked to Avenue Bernard and bought some chocolate and nuts. When I got back, the layering of the vocals sounded to me like a frat-house choir belting out a drinking song about ancient Greece. I left the vocal battle of "Achilles" for the mixing stage.

Meantime, I had some guitar overdubs to do. In the absence of Morey's virtuoso fretwork, I took matters into my own hands and recorded electric guitar solos for "Perfect Shell" and "Basement Rainbow," a droning part for "Cherries," and some minimalistic noodling on "Achilles." In several cases I was able to play through my Zoom device, colouring my (recently repaired) Gibson guitar with sounds found in the gizmo. I was pleased with the results.

There was time on the clock for one more item. I had hoped to be able to record "Grace of Love," but the chorus had kept morphing through various false starts over the past year. Just the previous day, I'd settled on an arrangement that incorporated no less than three choruses. I explained the situation to Bilerman, who wondered whether we might do a solo acoustic version of the song. I played it for him in the control room. He had a thought. An excellent drummer happened to be working upstairs; Bilerman called the guy. Within an hour, Dave Payant was behind the drum kit. We methodically worked out beats for the different sections of the song. Payant put his sticks aside and used brushes, and his energy powered the song like a gutsy, finely tuned engine. We did nine takes as the setting sun filtered through the frosted glass bricks.

The song was unfinished—fittingly for "Grace of Love," which had always been so resistant to completion—but this was nonetheless a positive note to end on. Payant's drumming provided the throbbing heart of the song. I slipped my guitar into its gig bag, said goodbye to Bilerman, and lugged away the black case that held Leon's accordion, which I was going to keep at home until he could pick it up. Maybe it would once again emit a tuneful sigh, planting the idea of a song in my head that would get recorded in twenty years' time.

CHORUS MAXIMUS

O N A COLD, WIND-WHIPPED morning, I arrived at a small detached home in a scruffy Toronto neighbourhood known as Junction Triangle. I had finally set up a recording session in Toronto with Rebecca Campbell. The plan was to get her to sing "Grace of Love," the last of my twelve songs that needed vocal closure.

I had asked Bilerman whether he knew of a place where I might record her vocals, and he'd put me in touch with his friend Gavin Gardiner, a singer-songwriter with a home studio. After arriving at Gardiner's house, I went around back to the stand-alone garage and, as instructed, phoned him to say I was outside. The green door to the garage soon opened, and a very tall, rangy man welcomed me into the studio. He sported a black toque, trim beard, and hair cascading past his shoulders.

My recording adventures had thus far taken place in a basement, an attic, and a "Hotel." It was fitting that a garage was now added to the mix. Once inside, I feasted my eyes on vintage guitars hanging from the walls, a sparkly brown drum kit, maroon oriental rugs, and framed salvaged signs with regulations like JEANS OR DENIMS NOT PERMITTED. There were no windows, and the effect was a self-contained alternate universe devoted to songcraft.

Gardiner fronts the roots rock band The Wooden Sky. He plays guitar, bass, and harmonica, among other instruments, and has a wonderfully deep singing voice. He also knows sound recording, having taught university-level courses in the field.

Three songs of mine, emailed by Bilerman, were sitting in Gardiner's Pro Tools recording system. The plan was for Rebecca to sing on top of songs that had been recorded in Montreal. In tech terms it was as easy as appending a paragraph to an email sent from another town. Gardiner, wearing a lumber jacket, took his seat behind his laptop and cued up "Grace of Love" so we could check that it was the right version.

"I really hear some tambourine on this," he said. "Tambourine is my favourite instrument."

"Right," I said.

"No, it really is," he said. "I love the tambourine."

"Well, I'm more than happy to have you lay down a tambourine track," I said.

The main reason for the session soon showed up. Rebecca, chilled from her ride over on bicycle, was wearing an Austin City Limits sweatshirt and a toque with red horizontal stripes. After some small talk in which she and Gardiner pinpointed musician friends they had in common, she took up her position at a microphone set up in a small closed-off area by the door, not much bigger than a telephone booth. She sang "Grace of Love" with a voice that was by turns soulful and twangy, her eloquent curlicues embroidering my straight-ahead melodic blueprint. Clutching a lyric sheet marked with her own notations, the singer had clearly done her homework.

"It's like Olivia Newton-John," Gardiner said to me at one point.

I gave him a dissatisfied look.

"Linda Ronstadt?" he tried.

After motoring through "Grace," Rebecca added a few lush coats of vocal harmonies. Halfway through the session, she and I took a break and walked through the biting cold to a soup joint for lunch, followed by some coffees at a diminutive café called Hula Girl. Soon we were back in Gardiner's garage. And very soon after that, we'd finished lead vocals and harmonies for two more songs, "Basement Rainbow" and "Perfect Shell," the latter rewritten for her preferred key. Her exquisite vocals were now indelibly stamped on all three songs.

"I haven't really sung lead on anything for a while," she said. "That was really fun!"

I thanked her profusely, we hugged goodbye, and the road-warrior singer got back on her bike to brave the fierce wind.

Afterwards, Gardiner did record some tambourine on "Grace of Love," and the two of us had a gas jamming with two tambourines on "Perfect Shell."

"I hear harmonica on this," Gardiner said regarding "Grace of Love." After rooting around for a harmonica in the right key, he recorded a full-throated solo, filling a hole that I hadn't until then figured out what to do with. After running out of time—he had a band rehearsal—I bid this friendly musical giant goodbye, on a very amiable note.

ONE WEEK LATER I was back in Hotel2Tango for what was to be my last session. The plan was to mix those three songs Rebecca had sung.

"You'll find this interesting," Bilerman said in the control room. "In fact it involves you. Remember that reel-to-reel you gave me?"

A couple of months earlier I'd given him the old eight-track reel-to-reel tape containing the recordings I'd made with Michael Leon two decades ago. Bilerman was kind enough to transfer the material to a digital format for me.

"I was recording this hardcore punk band," he said. "They're called Perfect Pussy."

"Perfect Pussy?"

"Yeah. They're from Syracuse and they're doing really well. They're getting a lot of buzz on the Internet."

He was using the same studio "rental reel" that he had used to digitize my ancient music, and thought he'd erased my old recordings. But at the end of one of Perfect Pussy's songs a strange "artifact" could suddenly be heard. It was in fact a voice. My voice, circa 1994, rendered at double speed and left by accident on the tape. The hardcore band had very much liked the weird coda.

"I told them that it belonged to this guy Eric and I'd have to get his permission for them to use it," Bilerman said. He played me a snippet of the music.

"Ha. I recognize the song. It was called 'The Whisky Priest.'"

I briefly wondered whether there was any reason not to allow the chipmunky, double-time version of my voice to form the outro of a song by a band called Perfect Pussy.

"You have my official permission," I said.

My voice could use all the exposure it could get. With Rebecca singing three songs now, my vocals had been reduced to two tunes out of the twelve. And much as I appreciated — worshipped, in some cases — the vocals of Michael Jerome Browne, Shaharah, Jo, Hayley, Michael Leon, and Rebecca, I was feeling ever so slightly elbowed out of my own project.

I couldn't have it both ways, of course; I couldn't have those fabulous singers showcase my songs and also have my own vocals, "authentic" and "unpretentious," as Bilerman once called them, remain in the tunes as part of my creative DNA. And yet...

Bilerman was mixing a new version of "Basement Rainbow" with Rebecca's voice. "I prefer you singing this," he said.

"Really?"

"Maybe I'm just used to it, but I like your version."

"But there's no contest. She's a singer. I'm not."

"I find that almost unanimously if someone is covering a song they over-sing it," said Bilerman. "I think that applies to your songs, and that's why for the most part I've said, 'No, Eric, I think your version is better because it just feels right.'"

We then mixed Rebecca's version of "Perfect Shell," which to my ear was still far better than the "author's cut." And we did a mix for the "unplugged" version of "Cherries." At an earlier mixing session, while working on the original version, the one with Morgan and Bucky and Ellwood Epps on trumpet and Jo playing organ, it had all started to feel busy to me. I'd had Bilerman strip away layer after layer until we were left with Jo's voice and my guitar, and it sounded plenty full. Almost stood on its own. Since then, I'd added some rhythm guitar and cello. Now, as we worked on the mix, I wondered about percussion. That's when Bilerman proceeded to do something that I would have thought out of character.

He played tambourine.

I was trying a run-through on tambourine when Bilerman suggested we trade places. He showed me how to operate the talkback system so I could communicate with the tracking room. And he showed me which button to click on the computer to start recording. Sitting on his ergonomic Aeron chair, feeling like a pilot on a very comfortable flight, I watched through the glass as Bilerman took a seat in the tracking room, donned headphones, and picked up the tambourine. When he said he was ready, I moved the cursor over to the Record button and clicked. Bilerman started slapping the tambourine against his thigh, head bent over prayer-like. With his glasses and serious mien, he cut the figure of a jingle-jangle Talmudic scholar, hypnotically one with the rhythm of the song. After seeing him at his observation post for so long, I found it satisfyingly topsy-turvy to view Bilerman through the studio glass as he rolled up his sleeves to play an actual instrument.

We later mixed "Grace of Love," which was decked out with Rebecca's exuberant vocals. Owing to the happenstance of who happened to be in the studio when the song— complete with drums, bass, guitar, cello, harmonica, and tambourine—had taken on a different complexion than I had ever imagined.

As Bilerman mixed, I was able to see him in his element. He zipped around on the wheels of his ergonomic chair, shuttling among the computer to his left, the stacks of outboard gear to his right, and the vast, multi-knobbed mixing board, with its rows of faders, spread out in front. He pushed and pulled cables in and out of the "patch bay" area like an old-fashioned Bell operator making telephonic connections. His expression was serious. His head swaying to the song's rhythm, he twisted and turned knobs, tweaking like mad, flicking faders up or down, moving with a nearly frantic energy. Then he would lean back on his chair to listen to what he'd just crafted, occasionally cupping his hands to each ear to isolate the intake of sound. All this, I realized, was Bilerman playing his instrument. From what I could hear, he was a virtuoso.

There was only one thing left to do. It was an afterthought, an indulgence, but something I'd decided would be worthwhile. I wanted to sing my own version of "Grace of Love." My guide track vocals didn't seem half bad. I could lay down my new vocals quickly, providing a tidy bookend to the whole twelve-song recording project. I remembered in great detail how I'd struggled to compose the song, how many incarnations it had gone through—the original verse (featuring lyrics about brushes with death) that I'd deleted on Jo's advice; the verse that became a chorus that I switched back into a verse; the pre-chorus that changed shape; and finally, on Morey's urging, my frenetic attempts at coming up with a bigger better greater chorus.

In the end, I found myself with no less than three different choruses—a *chorus maximus*. Under the deadline pressure of the last tracking session at H2T, I came up with an idea that employed all of those choruses (one as a sort of teaser, another as a bona fide chorus, the third as a bridge). Neither Jo nor Morey was helping me at that point. The deluge of choruses didn't seem to move them one way or another. After seeking their advice for so long on so many issues, I finally stopped caring about what they thought. I'd taken enough straw polls on my songs, buttonholed my mentor, bounced ideas off my sounding board, and wrestled with so many versions of my songs. I felt as if I'd learned enough. I went with my gut.

And my gut was telling me to sing the song. Rebecca's vocals on the tune were so strong that she took immediate ownership of it. But I wanted to sing my version. As I thought about it, I realized that I'd always wanted to sing my songs. It was a visceral need. That had been the songwriting lure for me since, as a thirteen-year-old, I'd penned my first tune with vocals about *flying on the ocean / swimming on the moon / and I'm still in love with you*. It stayed with me through my various phases in musical taste, my learning curve on guitar, and the changes in the technology of playing, listening, and recording music. I had a need to sing a song I'd written. Or to write a song I could sing.

Songwriting had never left me. This wasn't because I wanted to "make it," though had that possibility ever seemed the least bit likely, I would have jumped at the chance. I kept writing music because ideas would come to me while I played the guitar—emphasis on "play" here—and some notion of a complete and worthy song would come to mind. And then the visceral thing kicked in, the tactile, emotional need, quasi-sexual or athletic, like wanting to keep playing a sport when all your cylinders are firing in just the right way, wanting to keep playing like only a kid can want, or feel entitled to.

That's why I kept singing songs. On many occasions I might be intensely hungry, or en route to the bathroom, but I'd see my guitar and think of a song I was working on and delay that other bodily need. Just to partake in the energy of some melody that was churning within. Whether the need is biochemical or emotional or just a pleasurable way of avoiding real work, I have no idea. The desire is simply there.

That's the impulse that led me back to Hotel2Tango one last time. I wanted to sing "Grace of Love." In truth, I wanted to sing all my songs, even if I wasn't quite good enough. Listening to my old tunes, the ones that Bilerman had transferred from analogue tape recorded in the 1990s, it seemed to me that many of them were pretty solid constructions. My voice, on the other hand, was held together with duct tape and Popsicle sticks. You could argue that the singer-songwriter brings an authenticity to his or her songs, irrespective of how technically accomplished the voice happens to be; you could make the case that rock music has liberated vocals from conventional notions of what constitutes a good singing voice. But still, it was painfully clear to me that my voice was a drag on my songs. There are people who can sing words from a telephone book, just cruising on half-formed melodies, and they sound heavenly. It must feel nice.

Not that having a stellar voice is any guarantee in the music business. As impressive as Jo's, Shaharah's, Hayley's, and Rebecca's voices may have been, the industry was not knocking down their doors.

Jo's efforts at sending her music out to agents and record labels had not—to my surprise—led anywhere. Still, she wasn't throwing in the towel. "My plan," she told me, "is to write better songs. And you know what? To start playing live. At least once. To do something brave."

For Shaharah, her regular shows continued to give her—and her audiences—great pleasure. But for the time being, wider recognition had not materialized. Last we'd talked, she told me she'd gone back to university to finish the undergraduate degree that she'd started a decade earlier. She was taking English lit courses and thinking of going into communications or creative writing. Still, making music remained her priority. She had released a record on iTunes, and her latest plan was to record an album of the interpretations of R&B songs that she was detonating dance floors with.

Hayley Richman, who turned sixteen in 2015, had meanwhile declined Sony's offer of a development deal. Her father didn't quite see the point when Hayley was racking up such big numbers on the Internet. "We're up to 3.3 million views on YouTube," he told me. "More than thirty-two thousand subscribers to her YouTube channel—that's an insane amount. And it's going up by like six or seven thousand views per day." Add to that the fifty to seventy comments a day Hayley was getting on her fan page.

Morey and Hayley found themselves courted by a Los Angeles producer of Hollywood movie trailers, who wanted them to record some cover songs with the goal of getting their music into cinemas. And an accomplished filmmaker got in touch wanting to make a music video free of charge for one of their original songs. His first choice among their tunes was one called "Honey from the Sky."

As for that song, a grand total of seventy-three down-loads had been sold over the Internet on sites like iTunes. Although Morey seemed impressed with that figure, it struck me more as proof of how tough the record business is.

Still, despite the hurdles facing even such brilliant singers as these, my mind was made up. I was going back to the studio. I was going to sing one last song.

THE SOUND IN MY HEAD

T HE BEAUTY OF THE studio is that when all its sonic stars are aligned, when you've had a good night's sleep, and the engineer selects an optimum microphone, and the headphone mix sounds just right, and you haven't had one too many coffees, and sunshine filters through the glass brick wall in a soft, lyrical way, providing a kind of studio grace, you can hear yourself captured in the very best light.

It might mean having an engineer or a producer who pushes you, who urges you to try one more take, feeling that somehow you have it in you to do better. Or to tell you to quit on one of those days when it's just not happening. That's what Bilerman had told me during the sessions, when I'd taken my first stab at singing "Grace of Love."

"It sounds like, um, maybe you have a cold," he said.

Maybe I had been fighting congestion during that particularly brutal Montreal winter in early 2014. Or maybe the studio stars were not in place.

A couple of months later, I was back at H2T with one modest objective. I was going to sing "Grace of Love."

I expected a bit of sadness at the studio. A few nights earlier, I had heard Gavin Gardiner's band The Wooden Sky perform at a club in Montreal. Before the show, Gardiner was mingling with the audience, and we exchanged a few words.

"Howard is supposed to show up, but I don't know if he will," he said. "His dog died today."

"Gus?"

"Yeah."

"Oh, that's terrible. He was a great studio dog," I said.

"He was. I wish my dog was as good in the studio."

During his impressive performance, Gavin made mention of the in-house dog at Hotel2Tango. "This next song is for my friend Howard and for Gus," he said onstage.

Two days later, the morning was grey and rainy when Bilerman let me in through the heavy door of the studio, for what was supposed to be — yet again — my last session. He was wearing a five o'clock shadow, a lavender shirt, and a string bracelet.

"I heard about Gus from Gavin Gardiner," I said. "My condolences."

"He made a lot of good records, that dog," Bilerman said. He noted that Gus had lived to the age of fourteen years, eleven months. "He even got his barks on a few records."

Bilerman had already assembled a rough mix of "Grace of Love" in B-flat major. He set up a single mic so that I could record a guitar part for this version of the song. Within a few takes we had something. Then it was time for my vocals. I took several stabs, with mixed results. Back in the control room, Bilerman and I settled into a routine that was now very familiar.

"Are you worried about the bleed?" I asked, referring to the risk that my "guide vocals" and guitar from the original recording of the song had been picked up by the microphones on the drums. He wasn't worried. We listened to my lead vocals.

"It sounds like you're straining a bit," Bilerman said. "Try singing from your chest more."

"My chest? How?"

"More from your chest," he said, gesturing with one hand as if to strangle his throat, "than from up here."

I went back into the big tracking room and took another crack at "Grace," standing on the oriental rug and looking straight at the poster of the scantily-clad circus girl and the tiger. My voice felt good. I did a few run-throughs.

"Great," said Bilerman.

That evening, I listened to the mix at home. It wasn't great. The verses and pre-choruses sounded quite good. But the choruses — with me singing my own harmonies — sounded off. Quite off. Like maybe *Auto-Tuneable* off. I had failed again. The song was still not done.

A couple of weeks later, I was back at the Hotel. Bilerman was sporting a nasty gash on his forehead.

"I banged into a balcony," he explained. "I was talking on the phone. Arguing with a banker, in fact."

"Looks painful."

"It's not too bad. But you may notice the smell of muscle relaxant. So . . . what was it you wanted to redo on the song?

"The choruses," I said. "And the harmonica solo was too low in the mix. Everything else sounds great. I really like the sounds you got. But the choruses sound thin. Maybe a bit off-key. Maybe my own backups are getting in the way. I did a better job on the guide track vocals. Let's try to use those."

We spent about an hour working on the vocals. The choruses on the original guide vocals were fine; we placed those in the new mix, Bilerman thickening them a bit with the vocals I'd recorded during the previous "final" session. Then we found better versions of the bridge and the third verse of the song. And we boosted the harmonica solo.

"It all sounds good to me," Bilerman said. "I don't know what I'd change."

Bilerman put "Grace of Love" on a USB key with all the other songs I'd done, data that could one day be turned into CDs or vinyl records or digital downloads. Then, as a backup for me in case lightning were to strike Hotel2Tango, he transferred everything we'd done in the studio—every last take that had been recorded—to a small external hard drive.

After we packed up and Bilerman locked the various doors of the studio, I thanked him for all his efforts and gave him a farewell hug.

"I feel like I should congratulate you or something," he said.

I helped him pull the tarp off his Fiat, and he got into the old black roadster. I left on foot with my external hard drive, no bigger than a deck of cards, containing all the songs, remixes, alternative versions, and individual takes recorded at Hotel2Tango over the previous twelve months.

The next morning, I gave a listen to the latest mix—the one with the composer singing—of "Grace of Love." I cranked the volume on my home computer. The sound was down-to-earth, full, and swampy, a thick stew of instruments in B-flat major. It contained flavours I'd never anticipated during the many months I was banging away at the tune on acoustic guitar, desperately trying to come up with a better chorus. The wonderfully churning drums were everything I'd hoped for. The loping bassline and harmonica blasts and meandering cello gave the song depth and beauty. All the instruments sat nicely in the mix. And the singing voice was the sound that all along had been in my head.

LYRICS AND LINER NOTES

All lyrics by Eric Siblin

*All music by Eric Siblin except "Honey from the Sky,"
by Eric Siblin and Morey Richamn; and "Firewall,"
by Eric Siblin and Shaharah.*

PERFECT SHELL

All the way back
in the beginning
I had my ear to the ground
I heard you say that
all is forgiven
when there's beauty to be found

*It's over now—I see it in the hardness of your style
for what it's worth—you're dazzling, and you wear it well
you're a perfect shell*

Now's the season
of the hurricane
undercover enemies
there's no reason
there's no blame
just a restless energy

Waiting for the water
the tide will come in
it's over and done
when you disappear
once and for all
I'll come up for air
come out of my shell

Who appointed you
queen regent
of this patch of land
it's nothing new
always leaving
building castles in the sand

Lead Vocals, Rebecca Campbell; Drums, Bucky Wheaton; Bass, Morgan Moore; Acoustic and Electric Guitars, Eric Siblin; Organ, Jo Simonetti; Trumpet, Ellwood Epps; Backup Vocals, Rebecca Campbell; Tambourine, Gavin Gardiner. Recorded and mixed by Howard Bilerman at Hotel2Tango. (Vocals and harmonica recorded at Gavin Gardiner's home studio)

(Alternate version: Lead Vocals, Eric Siblin; Backup Vocals, Jo Simonetti)

GO SLOW

rhythm streets
glasses rhyme
new orleans
footnotes shine

I want to lift the burden from your eyes
make you see

Go slow if you must leave
I know we'll meet again
I will see you on the other side
be sure to leave a sign

dionysian
brass parade
you are breathing
ancient days

I want to turn the pages in your eyes
make you see

Go slow if you must leave
I know we'll meet again
I will see you on the other side
be sure to leave a sign

all the victories
in the field
cast in bronze
on your shield

Lead Vocals, Eric Siblin; Drums, Bucky Wheaton; Bass, Morgan Moore; Acoustic Guitar, Eric Siblin; Organ, Jo Simonetti; Trumpet, Ellwood Epps; Backup Vocals, Jo Simonetti. Recorded and mixed by Howard Bilerman at Hotel2Tango.

CHERRIES

Slowly you find yourself on top a saddle
a palomino that flies
sunshine beating time on the mountain
father rides by your side

Cherries will blossom when you give the word
all of this one day it will be yours
smoke rings lifting circle the sky
cherries will blossom tonight

Smoking a bedouin pipe in the desert
circles of grey fill the air
on the horizon an old cloud is waiting
the burnt offering you prepared

Driving an old car up to the schoolyard
workman's hands on the wheel
five o'clock shadows falling on gravel
poetry from the new world

Lead Vocals, Jo Simonetti; Acoustic and Electric Guitars, Eric Siblin;
Cello, Kristina Koropecki; Egg Shaker and Bass Tom, Bucky Wheaton;
Tambourine, Howard Bilerman. Backup Vocals, Jo Simonetti. Re-
corded and mixed by Howard Bilerman at Hotel2Tango.

(Alternate version: Drums, Bucky Wheaton; Bass, Morgan Moore;
Organ, Jo Simonetti; Trumpet, Ellwood Epps)

ACHILLES (UNABRIDGED)

Adapted from Homer's Iliad, *with the first two stanzas taken from Robert Graves's translation*

Sing through me that anger which
Ruinously inflamed Achilles,
Peleus' son,
And which, before the tale was done,
Glutted hell with champions—bold
Spirits by the thousandfold

Ravens and dogs their corpses ate
And thus did Zeus, who watched their fate,
See his resolve first taken when
Agamemnon, king of men,
An insult on Achilles cast,
Achieve accomplishment at last

Agamemnon the Greek king
Set in motion quarrelling
When respectful Chryses
The Trojan priest
Offered ransom desperately
To obtain his daughter's release

The anger of Achilles
Echoing to this day
The centuries forgive you
For putting down your sword and walking away

Agamemnon tempted fate
Don't let me see you here again
Among these hollow ships of war
No priestly headband will restore
Your daughter she must spend her life
As my royal concubine

The old priest, defeated,
Walked along the whispering sea
And offered up a bitter prayer
Apollo, Troy's protector, heard
Let the Greeks pay with arrows
For these burning tears of mine

Apollo heard the old man's plight
His face grew dark as the night
Shouldering his silver bow
Hurried down from the mount
Arrows rattled anger quaked
There came a fearful plague

Apollo's arrows they did fly
For nine straight days the funeral pyres
Burning everywhere
The Greeks gathered in despair
When the assembly met
Achilles took the sceptre and said:

What have we done to bring such fate
Upon our camp so mercilessly
We must consult prophet or priest

Or some interpreter of dreams
To see why some divinity
Has been offended by us Greeks

Calchas son of Thestor rose,
A prophet of all things unknown,
Carefully identified
The reason for Apollo's ire:
Agamemnon must return
The bright-eyed girl

Now Agamemnon he did rise
Anger flashing from his eyes
Surrender he would, if he must
His Trojan mistress
But some other Greek must provide
Him with a slave-girl prize

Achilles scowled at the king:
Shameless profiteering
Give up the woman
But leave us what we won
Fairly in warfare
While you took the lion's share

I did not join your force of arms
Because the Trojans did me harm
No cattle or horses they took from me
Or ravaged through my cornfields
I'm not here as your vassal
But of my own accord and Zeus's will

Across the misty mountain chains
The sea that surges far away
In Phthia
The land I love
I answered your call to war
As a favour, and nothing more

Ungrateful king, dog-faced wretch
My bravery you now forget,
How I led every last assault
And though you took most of the spoils
You now want my girl Briseis
Enough: I'll sail home to Phthia with dignity

Lead Vocals, Eric Siblin; Drums, Bucky Wheaton; Bass, Morgan Moore; Acoustic and Electric Guitars, Eric Siblin; Organ, Michael Leon; Backup Vocals, Michael Leon. Recorded and mixed by Howard Bilerman at Hotel2Tango.

BASEMENT RAINBOW

Pavement sky was overhead
sunshine on the ground
you and I together
ancient friends

You asked about children
curious for names
you never played the victim
never said why me

I'm still not over you
nothing could be farther from the truth you know
all our roads lead from a broken home
to a basement rainbow

Crystal chandeliers
a spinning dance floor
and on a clear day
we could see forever

Underneath the city stars
your architecture moved
I held you in my arms
trembling ruins

Lead Vocals, Eric Siblin; Drums, Bucky Wheaton; Bass, Morgan Moore; Acoustic and Electric Guitars, Eric Siblin; Accordion, Michael Leon; Backup Vocals, Jo Simonetti. Recorded and mixed by Howard Bilerman at Hotel2Tango.

(Alternate version: Lead Vocals and Harmonies, Rebecca Campbell)

BATTLEFIELD MIND

I was a lonely soldier
in a broken land of plenty
now there's a smoking crater
where a thing of beauty used to be

Floating on a mushroom cloud, watercolour greys
soft power fading now, showing my age
imaginary enemy lines
when the battlefield is on your mind

Such a sultry politician
in the back rooms of the strong
it was the smartest weapon
in the softest palm

You were defusing conflicts
in a lingerie disguise
you wore a true blue helmet
with your bulletproof bedroom eyes

I had my reasons for deserting
I was a free man and a slave
it was the season of forgetting
the calendar rearranged

Lead Vocals, Michael Jerome Browne; Drums, John McColgan;
Bass, Stephen Barry; Resonator Guitar, Michael Jerome Browne.
Recorded and mixed by Howard Bilerman at Hotel2Tango.

HONEY FROM THE SKY

I carried you
every step of the way
loving moves
feet of clay

I held you
every day
in my heart
a quiet flame

Sun coming up
honey from the sky
coming up for love
one last time

I was made for you
one part at a time
the engineer
knew the design

I saved you
from disaster
on a crayon river
in the hereafter

I helped you
pick up the pieces
the instructions
were all I needed

To put you
back together
reassemble
your true nature

Lead Vocals, Hayley Richman; Electric Guitars, Morey Richman; Backup Vocals, Hayley Richman; all other instruments programmed by Morey Richman. Produced and mixed by Morey Richman at his home studio.

COUNTRY MILE

I gave it my best shot, but it wasn't good enough
missed you by a country mile
every time I looked up, the cardinal was singing
I guess he will be silent for a while

Every night I reach out for a waiting hand
for a phantom limb that isn't there
so I turn to rapid eye playing deep inside
and your touch is always near

It's only natural to feel this way
I'll be the villain in a cowboy film
make it easier for you to walk away

Every strand of hair past sensation
precious treasures you left behind
I'm in the desert of your leaving
looking for empire in a grain of sand

I gave it lots of thought, but it tore me apart
miss you and I always will
wish I could build a bridge from me to you
made of silk and the strongest steel

Lead Vocals, Jo Simonetti; Drums, Eli Krantzberg; Bass, Peter
Wilson; Acoustic and Electric Guitars, Eric Siblin; Keyboards, Eli
Krantzberg. Recorded and mixed by Eli Krantzberg at his home
studio.

ANOTHER MAN'S CRIME

Pretty boy on a swivel chair
loosens his holster, says a prayer
somewhere on the Internet, kicking dust
he's looking for a password, looking tough

You're surrounded by zeros and ones
push of a button, kingdom come

Stuck inside another man's crime
nowhere to run in the dim light
stuck inside another man's crime

Pretty words, you're safe at home
sweet memories of Rosetta stone
somewhere in repairs, an old machine
has a broken hard drive, coming clean

You're surrounded by zeros and ones
push a button, kingdom come

Half alive with a gin and tonic
a crossword puzzle, a whodunit
sometimes with the blinding light playing tricks
even the weather is feeling fixed

A tiny lapse, caught on tape
and in a flash, no escape
somewhere there's a dragnet, getting tired
you call it in, on the wire

Stuck inside another man's crime...

Lead Vocals, Michael Leon; Drums, Eli Krantzberg; Bass, Peter Wilson; Acoustic and Electric Guitars, Eric Siblin; Keyboards, Steven Corber; Backup Vocals, Jo Simonetti. Recorded and mixed by Eli Krantzberg at his home studio.

(Alternative version: Lead Vocals, Shaharah)

FIREWALL

You're always flaming when you come up for air
I know you're on a mission to make yourself a victim
but I'm no longer able to care

Everybody gives you the time
ripped from your own headlines
you can only be seen when you are burning

Firewall — protection

You're always raging when you rise from the floor
I know you're just an ember until I remember
but I won't hold the match no more

Tinderboxes keep you alive
pyrotechnics always fly
you can only feel when someone sees you hurting

I know that gravity won't stop you
someone else will be there when you fall
I hope that you keep going till you are stopped once and
     for all

*Lead Vocals, Shaharah; Drums, Paul Lizzi; Bass, Greg Provo;
Electric Guitars, Eric Siblin; Keyboards, Ralph Télémaque; Saxophone, Erik Hove; Backup Vocals, Shaharah. Recorded and mixed
by Eli Krantzberg at his home studio.*

SIGN OF DESIGN

I'm looking
straight at you
for a sign of higher life
don't worry
it's nothing
that I can visualize

I'm waiting for an explanation
a rhyme or reason why
give me a theory
a sign of design

You're turning
the pages
of high-living magazines
you're learning
the hard way
how empty it all can be

Intelligent Design...

You're hearing
the footsteps
of gold-plated dinosaurs
I'm feeling
the sadness of
past present future

Lead Vocals, Shaharah; Drums, Paul Lizzi; Bass, Greg Provo; Electric Guitars, Eric Siblin; Keyboards, Ralph Télémaque; Backup Vocals, Shaharah. Recorded and mixed by Eli Krantzberg at his home studio.

GRACE OF LOVE

I was on an age-old track
the light was getting dimmer
star was swinging from your neck
signalling the maker

All the things connecting you
to the sky above
to the world outside

There but by the grace of love

A rapturous doctor
with oil-painting eyes
a virtuoso needle
is keeping you alive

All the things connecting you
to the sky above
to the world outside

By the grace of love go I
by the grace of love

The national anthem
the pearly-white smile
the gates of heaven approaching
the chariot ride

Lead Vocals, Rebecca Campbell; Drums, David Payant; Bass, Morgan Moore; Acoustic Guitars, Eric Siblin; Cello, Kristina Koropecki; Harmonica, Gavin Gardiner; Backup Vocals, Rebecca Campbell; Tambourine, Eric Siblin. Recorded and mixed by Howard Bilerman at Hotel2Tango. (Vocals and harmonica recorded at Gavin Gardiner's home studio)

(Alternate version: Lead Vocals, Eric Siblin)

All songs mastered by Harris Newman at Grey Market Mastering.

LINKS TO DRAMATIS PERSONAE

Stephen Barry: stephenbarry.bros.ca

Howard Bilerman: howardbilerman.com, http://www.ho-tel2tango.com/info.html

Blood and Glass: bloodandglass.com

Michael Jerome Browne: michaeljeromebrowne.com

Rebecca Campbell: rebeccacampbell.com

Steven Corber: ca.tm.org/web/montreal/contact-us

Ellwood Epps: ellwoodepps.blogspot.ca

Gavin Gardiner: thewoodenskymusic.com

Erik Hove: erikhovemusic.com, myspace.com/erikhove

Ralph Télémaque: raykeyz.com

Kristina Koropecki: markberube.com

Eli Krantzberg: elikrantzberg.com

Paul Lizzi: paullizzi.com

Morgan Moore: bloodandglass.com

Harris Newman: greymarketmastering.com

Ratspace Rehearsal and Recording Studio: ratspace.com

Hayley Richman: youtube.com/user/HayleyRichman

Shaharah: shaharah.com

Jo Simonetti: soundcloud.com/user220446067

The Tibaldos: thetibaldos.bandcamp.com

ACKNOWLEDGEMENTS

THIS BOOK AND THE music behind it are indebted to many people. Janie Yoon, my incisive editor, deserves much credit for pushing me to rewrite until a rambling manuscript was more or less in tune. Stalwart friends—Joel Simon, Ingrid Abramovitch, Daniel Sanger, and especially Mark Abley—gave invaluable feedback and saved me from countless gaffes. Morey Richman and Jo Simonetti enriched both the songs and the adventure of recording them. Many other musicians, whether pro bono pals or hired hands, made the studio sessions a multi-layered joy for me. Rebecca Campbell, Michael Leon, Shaharah Sinclair, Michael Jerome Browne, and Hayley Richman all were generous with their time and talent. Session musicians Morgan Moore, Bucky Wheaton, Ellwood Epps, Erik Hove, Kristina Koropecki, Peter Wilson, Paul Lizzi, Greg Provo, Steven Corber, Ralph Télémaque, and Dave Payant left me with fond memories and brilliant tracks.

Eli Krantzberg, Howard Bilerman, and Gavin Gardiner were kind-hearted virtuosos at the studio consoles. Harris Newman deftly handled the mastering of the songs. I am also grateful to all those at House of Anansi Press, including Sarah MacLachlan, Matt Williams, Emily Mockler, Laura Meyer, Gillian Fizet, Barbara Howson, and Carolyn McNeillie. Peter Norman provided stellar copyediting; Marian Hebb lent an expert hand with some legal fine print; and in the virtual sphere, I am very thankful to my friend James Taylor for designing the website that goes with this book, to be found at ericsiblin.com. The songs in the book can be streamed or (for book purchasers) downloaded free from the website. For free downloads enter the promo code: papyrus. The songs can also be purchased on iTunes and other Internet music sites.

My use of some proper names, which might appear haphazard, can be explained. I employed first or last names depending on which stuck in my head — ergo "Krantzberg" versus "Jo." As for street names in Montreal, for the most part I used English in largely Anglophone areas and French in Francophone parts of town; hence Sherbrooke Street West and Avenue du Mont-Royal.

A few sources should be singled out for helping me place my story in context. Greg Milner's *Perfecting Sound Forever: An Aural History of Recorded Music* was very happily read more than once. Additional background was gleaned from *Playback: From the Victrola to MP3, 100 Years of Music, Machines, and Money,* by Mark Coleman. And leafing through many issues of *Tape Op: The Creative Recording Magazine* (www.tapeop.com) provided some sound engineering enlightenment.

The source for the seventeenth-century epigraph at the start of this book is found in *Pleasures of Music*, edited by Jacques Barzun. Found in the same work is a quote by Virgil Thomson: "Nobody is ever patently right about music."